D1174991

Nay-Saying
in Concord

Emerson, Alcott, and Thoreau

Nay-Saying in Concord

Emerson, Alcott, and Thoreau

BY

T A Y L O R   S T O E H R

ARCHON BOOKS

Hamden, Connecticut

1979

© Taylor Stoehr 1979

First published in 1979 as an Archon Book,

an imprint of The Shoe String Press, Inc.

Hamden, Connecticut 06514

Library of Congress Cataloging in Publication Data

Stoehr, Taylor, 1931-
Nay-saying in Concord.

Includes bibliographical references and index.
1. Transcendentalism (New England).
2. Emerson, Ralph Waldo, 1803-1882 — Political and social views.
3. Alcott, Amos Bronson, 1799-1888.
4. Thoreau, Henry David, 1817-1862 — Political and social views.
5. United States — Intellectual life.   I.   Title.
B905.S75   170   78-25580
ISBN 0-208-01767-4

To John and Prue Dings

Contents

7

Acknowledgments

I wish to thank Mrs. F. W. Pratt and Mr. Gerald Savory for permission to quote unpublished letters and journal entries of Alcott and Lane. I am also grateful to the Fruitlands Museums and to the Harvard College Library for access to unpublished materials and permission to print. Parts of this book have appeared in other forms in the *Canadian Review of American Studies* and in *ESQ,* to the editors of which I am indebted. I owe much to conversations with Jonathan Bishop and Neil Hertz, Chip and Susan Planck, Evelyn Barish, the late Alfred R. Ferguson, and my wife Ruth Perry. Most of all I talked it out with my loyal friends John and Prue Dings.

Introduction

Reform, people hate the sound of, now that they have begun to think it is like reading novels, which, when they are done, leave them just where they were, carpenters, & merchants, & debtors, & poor ladies, — only, they disbelieved the novel & believed at first the reformer.

Emerson's *Journals*

It has been a favorite complaint against the transcenden-talists to say that they had no adequate conception of evil — for which one must go to *The Scarlet Letter* and *Moby-Dick.* To be sure, these works glow with an infernal light not to be found in *Nature* or *Walden,* if that is the criterion. Since we have now become addicted to the public vice and private exculpation that Emerson condemned in "Man the Reformer" ("Every body partakes, every body confesses . . . yet none feels himself accountable"),[1] it is natural for us to respond more sympatheti-cally to writers who do not avert their faces from us. But at a deeper level I think the true source of our preference for "facing the evil" in life is the appeal of the fictive mode of consciousness itself. While we accuse the transcendentalists of priggishness, what we really object to is their failure to write narrative. Their works seem to us dull encyclopedias of admonition and good cheer. We are devotees of another use of the romantic imagina-tion. No need for me to catalogue its plots and machinations; these forbidden desires and mythic satisfactions are more

13

familiar to us than our native streets. It could be shown that the nature of such visions must be a revelation of evil, but this is not the place for that argument. In any case, we dwell among such dreams, fantasies, and fictions to an extent unparalleled in the history of cultures.

The transcendentalists shared Hawthorne and Melville's view that their society was corrupt, but equally thrown back upon themselves, they treated consciousness as a therapy rather than a solace. The transcendentalists never stopped hoping to make life conform "to the pure idea" in their minds. The novelists made a pact with existence, agreed to live in the everyday world however it offered itself, so long as they might live, also, in their fantasies.

Later in this book I will present a detailed account of the transcendentalists' love of secluded hideaways, when discussing their reactions to invitations to live in the communities at Brook Farm and Fruitlands. It is interesting that Hawthorne, himself a former Brook Farmer, also had his "hut" in Concord — a cupola-study added to the top of the house that he bought from Bronson Alcott — but he descended to his family dinner each day more wholeheartedly than the transcendentalists ever did. By the same token, Emerson and Alcott never left human companionship so completely behind when they went to their studies in the morning. Hawthorne could draw the curtain between life and art; Emerson always felt uncomfortable, at odds with himself, in both — the one only real, the other only perfect.

This pact with existence is the subject of much of Hawthorne's best writing: the relations between consciousness and reality, and the impossibility of living in both, except through the fictive imagination. His heroes — Aylmer, Holgrave, Coverdale — begin with the hope of the transcendentalists, to make reality match the vision their imagination paints; but each discovers that such visions are damned. It is not the desire that is evil, but the attempt to realize it; for this is blasphemy (the sin of the artist). Hawthorne drew his moral explicitly: renounce such intentions, and be satisfied with an imperfect world. Such is the "realistic" view of evil that has shouldered out the transcendentalists in modern estimations.

For their part, the transcendentalists thought that novels were more or less despicable. Their sporadic samplings of Jane Austen and Dickens were rarely matters for congratulation; they came away as one comes away from the experience of watching television, vaguely defiled. I think this reaction was a revulsion from what they felt to be an abuse of the imagination. The abuse consisted in abandoning the attempt to make thought bear on life. *Walden* was equally a work of the imagination — what purer? — but it not only grew from experience (as did *The Blithedale Romance* and *Typee*), it also forced the reader back into experience; it called for action, if only the act of assimilating its reality to our reality, sharing Thoreau's consciousness. Novels do not ask this. It is the very premise of fiction that it leave our daily lives alone. Novels offer distance — a respite from reality, sometimes a comment on it, but most characteristically a representation of it. One may be deeply moved by such imaginings, but that is not the point. They never require anything of us. Prophecy is alien to them.

In the United States and most of the West, we have increasingly relied on a panoply of public media — fiction, cinema, television, sports events, popular music, drugs — to provide consciousness something to expend itself upon without disturbing the balance of practical realities. Our arts, our recreation, even our ceremonies have been commandeered. This is no mere imposition on modern society, of course, but an effect of social evolution, part and parcel of urbanization, bureaucratic centralism, and the division of labor carried to its technological apotheosis. Consciousness, like language, is distinctively human, and almost as old as upright posture; only in modern times has it become problematic, a burden, an issue. If in the nineteenth century, as Emerson said, "young men were born with knives in their brain,"[2] it was because the world was becoming less a sphere of action and more a perplexity.

At some point in the middle of the nineteenth century America was offered three choices: that of the communitists, that of the transcendentalists, and that of the novelists. We chose the last.

I will have more to say about the communitist attitude in another chapter, when I come to consider how far the transcendentalists could agree with its aims and methods, and why they ultimately preferred their solitary studies, summerhouses, and huts to the common rooms and dormitories of Brook Farm and other utopias. For the moment I merely want to locate communitism as one kind of response to the crisis in American society in order to give some context for the other two major responses, those of the transcendentalists and of the novelists, the yea-sayers and the nay-sayers as they have been called.

In the 1840s there were dozens of reforms competing for the honor of naming the root of society's evil and putting the axe to it — abolitionism, Grahamism, phrenology, prison and asylum reform, temperance, pacifism, compulsory education, women's rights, land reform, workingmen's association, and so on — but the reform of reforms, the one that came closest to representing if not actually combining all of these *isms* and *ologies*, was the communitist movement, which in a single decade produced scores of new utopian colonies across the country, explicitly establishing a total alternative to the corrupt society that other reformers were attacking piecemeal. We can now trace how many of these piecemeal reforms found their way into ordinary life, while little of the radical solution of communal life managed to establish itself. Here I am not so much concerned with these practical results as I am with the kind of spiritual response to society's ills the communitist movement offered. It too was basically reformist. The aim was to find new principles of organization, new structures, in which citizens might live and work more equitably and happily. Many of the methods we are familiar with today were then in fashion, especially the use of publicist techniques to gain adherents, and organizing techniques to control and wield power. The communitist attitude, whether manifested in actual colonies or merely in the "movement politics" of abolitionism, feminism, and the like, involved the development of group solidarity and the identification of the individual with the group will.

Let us keep in mind that the times were, in many places, revolutionary. While socialists in Europe prepared for 1848, abolitionists for 1860, and religious evangelists for the millennium, the transcendentalists worked at their revolution. It is worth repeating Emerson's formulation of 1842, in the first of a series of lectures "on the times": "The revolutions that impend over society are not now from ambition and rapacity, from impatience of one or another form of government, but from new modes of thinking, which shall recompose society after a new order, which shall animate labor by love and science, which shall destroy the value of many kinds of property, and replace all property within the dominion of reason and equity."[3] Perhaps it seems a bloodless rebelliousness, in more than one sense, that speaks of "modes of thinking" rather than barricades. Emerson had no faith in violence or its tactics. When he found himself literally on the scene in 1848, during a long visit to England, he noted in his journal: "People here expect a revolution. There will be no revolution, none that deserves to be called so. There may be a scramble for money. But as all the people we see want the things we now have, & not better things, it is very certain that they will, under whatever change of forms, keep the old system."[4] Such thoughts did not mean that he lacked sympathy with "Chartists & Montagnards," only that he would not be satisfied with a mere change of personnel in seats of power. "All spiritual or real power makes its own place. Revolutions of violence then are scrambles merely."[5]

The "revolutionary thinkers" Emerson preferred were described more fully in the rest of his "Lectures on the Times," especially in "The Transcendentalist": "They are lonely; the spirit of their writing and conversation is lonely; they repel influences; they shun general society; they incline to shut themselves in their chamber in the house, to live in the country rather than in town, and to find their tasks and amusements in solitude."[6]

These men seem far from the modern conception of radical activists. They were scarcely social, let alone comradely. The "speculative habit" appeared to use up the social energies; or perhaps it was that social intercourse dissipated consciousness. In any case, it disturbed the transcendentalists to discover that the closer one approached the ideal of social life advocated by the communitists, the more the imaginative life seemed to recede. Again Emerson reported: "the experience of the colleagues of Brook Farm was unanimous, 'We have no thoughts.'"[7]

With their "new modes of thinking" the transcendentalists had no interest in transforming society in the way that utopian experimenters intended — by means of the rational division of labor or the abolition of private property, for example. Nor was most transcendental political writing directed toward a public in the ordinary sense. Other reformers, like the temperance man, the Grahamite, or the abolitionist, tried to enlist audiences in their enthusiasms. But transcendentalist eloquence was less a matter of propaganda than of prophecy. One kept a journal in order to be in touch with the universe, not to control it. Whatever meaning nature and experience held could only be achieved by awareness, and perfected by meditation. Life = meaning = consciousness.

Even these lessons were not to be proclaimed so much as exemplified or enacted. Emerson's friend Bronson Alcott thought one need only find the right formula, the correct expression of the truth, and it would be immediately apparent to all. There would be no argument, only instant conviction. That was the idea behind his "orphic sayings." Emerson himself had written, at the end of *Nature,* in his guise as "Orphic poet": "Build, therefore, your own world. As fast as you conform your life to the pure idea in your mind, that will unfold its great proportions. A correspondent revolution in things will attend the influx of the spirit. So fast will disagreeable appearances, swine, spiders, snakes, pests, mad-houses, prisons, enemies, vanish; they are temporary and shall be no more seen."[8]

If one complained that it was a long time to wait for such results, Emerson, speaking again in the assumed voice of "the transcendentalist," had this answer:

> "What will you do, then?" cries the world.
> "We will wait."
> "How long?"
> "Until the Universe rises up and calls us to work."
> "But whilst you wait, you grow old and useless."
> "Be it so: I can sit in a corner and *perish*, (as you call it,) but I will not move until I have the highest command. If no call should come for years, for centuries, then I know that the want of the Universe is the attestation of faith by this my abstinence."[9]

In the chapters that follow I devote much attention to the notion of "revolutionary abstinence," especially as manifested in Alcott and Thoreau. Although Emerson was the least abstemious of the three, it is well to notice at the outset that he too could conceive of his faith as a form of abstinence. Whatever their differences, it is their shared vision that makes us want to consider them side by side. Compared to the communitists and other reformers, the transcendentalists are like a band of monks sitting cross-legged on the floor, indistinguishable in their chant.

The transcendentalists lived during the last years in America when it seems to have been possible to separate the opportunities of civilized life from its dangers, by means other than catastrophe. Therefore they were bold and self-assured, in works like "Man the Reformer," "Politics," "Life Without Principle," and "Resistance to Civil Government." At the same time they were already victims of the disease, "speculatists" as one friend called them,[10] purists of consciousness unwilling to live in a "double faced equivocating mixed Jesuitical uni-

19

verse."[11] It is this withdrawal to the mind's refuge, this washing one's hands of the clay, that seems least attractive in the transcendentalists. They achieved faith by closing down rather than opening up. It was not even a matter of relinquishing — nothing so openhanded as that.

Yet there is something to be said for this sacrifice of comfort and geniality. As they took it, the problem was how to live. Especially, how to live in the venal society they found themselves part of, not merely imperfect but sinning and forsworn. Shakers and other perfectionists had their own forms of abstinence and affirmation to offer as an answer — regeneration through love and social purity — but as we will see, the transcendentalists were unwilling to sacrifice their thoughts to what seemed to them at best a blessed oblivion. Neither did they wish to sink into the mesmerized acquiescence that they saw their neighbors and fellow citizens gradually settling for, treadmills of fantasy to absorb the unwanted energies of men who have shed their arms and legs, as Alcott predicted, and become all "brain."[12] (Let it be said that our extraordinary indulgence of the imagination has sometimes served us well — and not only for the sake of art. But here we are speaking of the price exacted.)

Melville once told Hawthorne that he was a great naysayer — said "NO! in thunder"[13] — and ever since the first literary historian stumbled on the phrase, the novelists have been celebrated as the heroic deniers and refusers, leaving the transcendentalists to fill the opposite role of optimistic applauders and yes-men. This is a false dichotomy. The truth is that Emerson, Alcott, and Thoreau, rather than say aye or nay, were more likely to abstain entirely. Theirs was the most conservative attitude of all, neither approving nor rejecting but simply awaiting the outcome — as their Eastern philosophers would say it, standing out of the way. The universe could be trusted to unfold without taking a vote.

Their position can be aptly illustrated by comparison with a few of Melville's characters: they were unwilling to fall back on the social contract, as Captain Vere finally does, for the grounding of reality; but equally adverse to the monstrous egotism of Captain Ahab, who demands some ultimate proof of his own existence. The transcendentalists aspired to the innocence of Billy Budd, to find a way of living their affirmation, deeper than speech, and only in extremity to stammer out some act of refusal. As Emerson pointed out when Thoreau refused his taxes, one could not keep oneself pure from all complicities with evil — you would end up renouncing the very bread in your mouth, the air in your lungs. But that was the transcendental impulse. Thoreau's example is famous; Alcott's also deserves to be, when at the demise of his colony at Fruitlands he took to his bed and refused all sustenance, resolving to die the death of Bartleby, the philosopher of noncomplicity.

It is important to notice how differently these exemplary acts affect us, depending on their origin in a novelist's imagination or in the course of an actual life. One can return again and again to Melville's fiction, always to be moved; he is doubtless our greatest novelist. But, because they are facts, Thoreau's night in jail and his two years in the woods have an even deeper power over the imagination, passing into myth as what is merely invented in a story cannot. This power has given Thoreau an extraordinary reputation and influence in our own times, in spite of the general shriveling of our imaginative life to the dimensions of the TV screen. If any of the transcendentalists has fulfilled Emerson's prediction, Thoreau is certainly the one whose "new modes of thinking" have proved more revolutionary than the intervening "scrambles" for political control.

My purpose in writing this book is to examine the sources of this mythic power more closely, to consider the facts themselves more fully and in their relevant contexts, and to ask what sort of eloquence it was that the transcendentalists struggled to achieve, what the relations of saying and doing amounted to in their experience, and what models for us may still be viable in their revolutionary abstinence and purist ideals. I do not wish to argue that they have covered all the ground for us, or provide ready-made answers. It will be enough if their examples help us see our own choices more clearly, and give us heart.

"Eloquence Needs No Constable"

A. or B. refuses the tax or some tax with solemnity, but eats & drinks & wears & perspires taxation all day. Let them not hew down the state with axe & gunpowder, but supersede it by irresistible genius; huddle it aside as ridiculous & obsolete by their quantity of being. Eloquence needs no constable.

Emerson's *Journals*

1. Private Discourse

Margaret Fuller's death by drowning in 1850 made an epoch in the history of transcendentalism. Having only just begun to gird themselves to face a new Margaret — she was coming home from Europe a wife and mother, under circumstances that made them anticipate still more drastic alterations — her friends were suddenly called upon to recollect and enshrine the old Margaret instead. In so doing, they found themselves reconsidering their own careers up to the arbitrary point marked by her death.

In his portion of the collaborative *Memoirs* that resulted, William Henry Channing opened by reminding his readers of the transcendentalist quarrel with established institutions — "the church, the state, the college, society, . . . even reform associations." Traditional organs of literary and political expression were no longer respected. Even *The Dial*, of which both Fuller and Emerson served as editor, had not been an adequate resonator for the new voices. "The journal, the letter, became of greater worth than the printed page."[1] Not that Fuller hadn't published a good bit in her short life, but everyone agreed that the best of her had never gotten into print — nor, for that matter, could it be recovered now, in her letters and journals, though these were the most authentic remains. Emerson spoke for them all in his section of the *Memoirs* when he wrote that her "powers and accomplishments found their best and only adequate channel in her conversation," and James Freeman Clarke quoted her to the same effect: "Conversation is my natural element. I need to be called out, and never think alone, without imagining some companion."[2]

As Channing suggested, Fuller's propensities were more or less those of her transcendentalist comrades. This can be seen, for example, in the last issue that she edited of *The Dial* (April 1842), where she published the following among numerous passages from the diaries of Bronson Alcott:

> Conversation
>
> . . . Sincerity in thought and speech can alone redeem man from this exile and restore confidence into his relations. We must come to the simplest intercourse — to Conversation and the Epistle. These are the most potent agencies — the reformers of the world. The thoughts and desires of men wait not thereby the tardy and complex agencies of the booksellers' favor, printers' type, or reader's chances, but are sped forthwith far and wide, by these nimble Mercuries. Christianity was published solely by the lip and pen, and . . . thus shall the New Ideas find currency in our time and win the people to themselves.[3]

What purer illustration could be found? A call for more intimate modes of address, itself framed as a diary entry, and published in an esoteric journal whose readers were chiefly its contributors and potential contributors, edited by a woman famous for her "conversation"; the call itself issued by a man who wished to be famous for *his* conversations, and whose "orphic sayings" were already a byword.

All such circumstances aside, Alcott's manifesto might sound like sour grapes. It would be tempting to attribute his dissatisfaction with booksellers to his own failure to write anything salable. Emerson's advice was against publishing "Psyche," Alcott's magnum opus of 1838 ("it disheartened me from taking my pen, for years afterwards, beyond my Diary"),[4] and although he enjoyed a certain notoriety through Elizabeth Peabody's *Record of a School,* in 1842 the *Conversations on the Gospels* that he printed as sequel to the *Record* had to be sold to the trunkmakers by the pound (nine hundred pounds at five cents per pound).[5] No doubt these factors played some part in Alcott's enthusiasm for the "nimble Mercuries" of private discourse; nonetheless, the upshot bore him out, for all his success — both among his intimates at the time and with the public some twenty years later — was as a conversationalist.

The transcendentalists were all of them famous for one or another variety of eloquence, but the truth is that they were not really avant-garde in their doctrine of spontaneous utterance. The age was right on their heels. In his diary Alcott made a little chart that suggests the broader outlines of the movement toward more direct modes of popular discourse:

> Garrison made the Convention
> Greeley made the Newspaper
> Emerson made the Lecture,
> and
> Alcott is making the Conversation.[6]

Who, one might ask, made the Epistle? Perhaps that was Margaret Fuller, Emerson's favorite correspondent — since Alcott claimed the Conversation for his own. Daniel Webster had surely made the Ceremonial Speech, Charles G. Finney just as surely the Evangelical Call, Fanny Wright instigated the Plea for Women's Rights, Andrew Jackson Davis the Trance-lecture, Oliver Wendell Holmes the Toast, and so on. Of course there were other contenders for each category; it was very much an age of discourse, and the transcendentalists were different only in regarding themselves as specialists in the more private forms of address.

One could argue that the declamatory impulse of the age was evangelical, witness the high proportion of ministers and ex-ministers among the new oracles. The last "great awakening" might be said to have succeeded, once and for all, in leading ministers as well as their congregations out of the conventional churches with their pat sermons and into the fields of inspirational speaking. Thus the last loud gasp of revivalism — Mormons and Millerites — was scarcely audible amidst the racket of countless other come-outerisms, from the truculent abolitionist improvisations of Abby Kelley and Stephen Foster to the spiritualist rhapsodies of Andrew Jackson Davis. Traveling agents for the New England Anti-Slavery Society took the place of circuit riders, conventions supplanted tent meetings, but impassioned speech gave rise to ecstatic conversion in the old way.

Similarly in more conservative circles the preacher might become a lecturer on the lyceum platform, opting for the congregation-at-large, and a wider range of topics. This was Emerson's choice, for example, and he explained it to his friend Carlyle: "I find myself so much more and freer on the platform of the lecture-room than in the pulpit, that I shall not much more use the last; and do now only in a little country chapel at the request of simple men to whom I sustain no other relation than that of preacher. But I preach in the Lecture-Room and then it tells, for there is no prescription. You may laugh, weep, reason, sing, sneer, or pray, according to your genius. It is the new pulpit, and very much in vogue with my northern countrymen."[7]

As fast as old institutions faded, new ones filled their places. Often the empty shell was taken over by a more vital organism; thus the old religious "anniversary weeks" of the churches in Boston and New York became a forum for radicals and publicists of every persuasion. Most important was the development of the lyceum system as a sort of secular ministry, with houses of edification in every center of population; by 1839 there were 137 lyceums in Massachusetts alone, some of them offering weekly lectures to audiences of thousands.[8] This network of mechanics' institutes, mutual education associations, and literary athenaeums began as scattered self-help in the 1820s and transformed itself into a lecture circuit in time for Emerson, Theodore Parker, Horace Greeley, and even Henry Thoreau to profit by it. In the early days popular science was its enthusiasm, then the pseudosciences — phrenology, mesmerism, hydropathy — and finally the new social sciences — associationism, individual sovereignty, and other philanthropies and panaceas. With the approach of the Civil War, slavery more and more became the overriding symbol of what was wrong with American society, and like every other public platform the lyceum was gradually converted to propaganda and rabble-rousing.

From the very beginning the most earnestly evangelical wing of the antebellum reform movement was abolition. The eloquence of antislavery orators was proverbial: it was "dog-cheap," said Emerson admiringly.[9] As a student of the art himself, and one who had left the ministry to avoid speaking as a hireling, Emerson might be expected to sympathize with the abolitionist endeavor. But his attitudes were never so uncomplicated as that. At least until the Fugitive Slave Act, abolition remained a problematic crusade for him. The basic ethical questions were clear enough, but the matter of tactics and zeal was in doubt. Consider his own stance as a purveyor of truths: he valued the freedom that lecturing gave him to choose his own topics without regard to the feelings of a congregation or constituency. Giving up his pulpit allowed him to "say at Public Lectures & the like, those things which I have meditated for their own sake & not for the first time with a view to that occasion."[10] For a man who wished to make every occasion a test of himself as much as his audience, this was a crucial condition of speaking. The electric effect of orators like Garrison and Phillips came from no such freedom to choose their subject, but from *its* choosing *them*, a "call" in the traditional sense. As Emerson remarked in his journal, not without a certain awe, "An advantage shines on the abolition side that these philanthropists really feel no clog, no check from authority, no discord, no sore place on their own body which they must keep out of sight or tenderly touch. People just out of the village or the shop reason & plead like practised orators, such scope the subject gives them, & such stimulus to their affections." Emerson pursued the implications for a tender conscience like his own: "Reason is glad to find a question which is not, like Religion or Politics, bound around with so many traditions & usages that every man is forced to argue unfairly, but one on which he may exhaust his whole love of truth, — his heart & mind."[11] Here is the classic temptation of those radicals who demand absolute purity of themselves in all things political, yet who see the inevitability of compromise in any practical and immediate solution. Men like Garrison inspired awe because they seemed never to make allowance for human failing, in either themselves or others.

Cynical as Americans have always been about rhetoric, especially political rhetoric, the great disillusionment was only just beginning in the days of Daniel Webster's infamous betrayal of his constituency, not to say humanity, when he voted for the Fugitive Slave Act. Audiences of the 1840s still wanted to believe in their spokesmen, whatever allowances they were learning to make for party and principles. Webster had been a hero of eloquence for New Englanders, before they caught him talking out of both sides of his mouth. Of course abolition was both a political and a religious question, as Emerson well knew before he was done with it. He had been among Webster's most admiring listeners; he was one of the first to execrate him in 1850. In such turnabouts and ambiguities one can see some of the difficulties of the transcendentalist position. Even Garrison was not wholly exempt, in Emerson's view, from the need to establish his truth "by the continual eye to numbers, to societies. Himself is not enough for him."[12] Public speech implied a desire to win an audience over to some viewpoint or action, and this in turn tempted speakers to adjust their words, and sometimes their opinions, to the prejudices of the masses. One might as well stay in the pulpit. Although Garrison certainly could not be accused of softening his language for any expediency, there was a strain of fanaticism at his core that grated on Emerson's genial nature. Even more than the venality of State Street, the evangelical temperament repelled him — so much so that Alcott reported him as saying that he "could never speak handsomely in the presence of persons of G[arrison]'s class."[13] Wendell Phillips was even less attractive, "only a *platform*-existence, and no personality." Emerson had no desire to meet him, however impressed he was by his eloquence. "They are inestimable for workers on audiences; but for a private conversation, one to one, I much prefer to take my chance with that boy in the corner."[14]

Obviously this ambivalence was grounded elsewhere than in the classical argument over the political abuses of rhetoric, though we shall see that the resolution finally imposed by history came from politics. The issues might just as well be posed in less partisan terms. During this period, for example, Emerson's journals are full of uncertainty over the claims of spontaneous speech and deliberate compositon, and the experience of being both a successful lecturer and a popular essayist was having its repercussions in his style. The alternatives were entangled with other concerns that went still deeper — not merely the comings and goings of inspiration or the laws of consciousness and will, but even his guiltiest misgivings about his relation with his family and friends.

In general Emerson appears to have been less comfortable and articulate in company than alone. If Garrison froze his powers, he was stiff even with his closest friends; Margaret Fuller told him that "she waits for the Lectures seeing well after much intercourse that the best of me is there."[15] Such blunt testimony might touch the quick, in the way that Margaret's candor often did, but even taken to heart, it was not advice that could settle the relations between extemporaneous and considered discourse. Suppose he was at his best as a talker when

31

he had a script in front of him ... just as there was a kind of speech that was totally composed, so there was a kind of writing that was impromptu. "When I write a letter to any one whom I love, I have no lack of words or thoughts: I am wiser than myself and read my paper with the pleasure of one who receives a letter, but what I write to fill up the gaps of a chapter is hard & cold, is grammar & logic; there is no magic in it; I do not wish to see it again."[16] One might quote another dozen passages to point up the conflict Emerson must have felt, and yet there is something in these contradictory formulations that remains consistent. "Wiser than myself," "the best of me," "the muse returns" — as the problem of eloquence came into focus for Emerson, it raised all the cherished transcendental questions about self, other, and consciousness, in a context of unresolved anxiety about his own sociability.

"In perfect eloquence," he wrote in the same notebook, "the hearer would lose the sense of dualism; of hearing from another; would cease to distinguish between the orator & himself; would have the sense only of high activity & progress."[17] This was not a state Emerson often, if ever, attained, but it was something he thought about quite seriously. In its most general formulation, the idea was a version of the apocalyptic optimism at the end of *Nature,* where he imagines the vanishing of snakes, pests, and madhouses before an "influx of the Spirit." Another time he framed the thought in more or less political terms: "There is for every man a statement possible of that truth which he is most unwilling to receive, a statement possible, so pungent & so ample that he cannot get away from it, but must either bend to it or die of it. Else, there would be no such word as eloquence, which means this."[18]

Whatever its varieties, this faith in words was an axiom among the transcendentalists. When they read one another's journals, they found their own ideas of eloquence anticipated. Emerson copied the following from Alcott's journal into his own: "Successful preaching implies, I imagine, the utterance of profoundest truth in simple phrase, touching the common sense of every one [—] the child, & adult, & being, at the same time, a pure model of eloquence both in tho't & expression ...."[19] It was about this time that Emerson was telling Alcott that his writing was too mannered for publication, a series of mystical pulsations, as Alcott admitted, "knit loosely together by the subtle threads of association felt only by myself."[20] But this was the very essence of his theory of "orphic sayings," the attempt in a few sentences to reach an intensity of speech that would go directly to the heart of his hearers. In a periodical appropriately titled *The Plain Speaker,* Alcott at once explained and exemplified what he had in mind:

Candor

The frankest speech, address most direct, proffered in meekness and love, is the reformer's only weapon. Men forthwith surrender in confessions. None can confront or withstand; their armor falls at once from their limbs, and they are won by manners thus magnanimous, humane. — The candid are crowned sovereigns of the world.[21]

One need only think of Garrison being dragged through the streets of Boston by an angry mob to see how far these ideas of eloquence were from the practical exigencies of reform.

Alcott's orphic voice had few hearers to surrender their weapons. Nonetheless, for local and private purposes Emerson thought him a "majestic converser," and even Thoreau was ready to welcome his loquacious "winter visitor" to his retreat by the pond.[22] In later years Alcott became a professional "converser," undertaking annual tours of the western states, where he was paid to talk in parlors with select companies of the like-minded. Although never much of a livelihood, it allowed him to maintain his self-respect as a radical — a man with a message. "Conversation" was perhaps the wrong word for Alcott's performances, for he seems to have used his interlocutors chiefly to prime his own pump. By 1874 Alcott had come to refer to his itinerary as "my bishoprick,"[23] a clue to his conception of his role, more like holding court than leading a discussion. He was "an inestimable companion," Emerson thought, "because he had no obligations to old or new; but is free as if new born. But he is not careful to understand you. If he gets a half meaning that serves his purpose, 'tis enough."[24] Emerson tried to put a good face on it: "He hardly needs an antagonist, — he needs only an intelligent ear." It is only fair to add that Alcott never pretended to value conversation for what somebody else might say — the "Touch-&-go" that Emerson would have preferred.[25] Alcott sought inspiration for his own uses. He aspired to "the miracles of eloquence" which Emerson said "can only be expected from the man who thinks on his legs."[26] Apparently Alcott was sometimes such a man, but the miracles did not always appear. When they did not, "tedious archangel" was a better name for him than "majestic converser," and Emerson did not hesitate to apply it, too.[27]

During the first years of their friendship it looked as if Emerson were going to regard Alcott as a prophet — a voice that would speak to his soul — so lavish are his journals in Alcott's praise, especially praise of his conversation. One assumes that Emerson must have been rather desperate to hear some such voice. Why else settle for this one, to which other ears, including those of Emerson's friends, seemed almost unanimously deaf (it "might make one despair of society," he sighed).[28] It must also be said that if Emerson had such a need, he soon recovered from it, and thereafter tended to treat Alcott more like a pet philosopher than the voice of truth. Before long he had fathomed the "trick" of Alcott's method — "which may be soon learned by an acute person & then that particular style be continued indefinitely. This is true of . . . all such specialists or mystics."[29] Still, there was certainly a time in the mid-1830s when Emerson was so taken with Alcott's eloquence as to drift toward discipleship, and even a dozen and more years of habituation to his friends's oracular manner did not deaden the music. More than any other man, it was Alcott on whom Emerson relied for inspiration. That was the secret of their friendship.

It was disappointing that Alcott had so little to show for his efforts and genius — no books, no following, no income. Emerson weighed him in the same balance that he used for all men. After many attempts he finally abandoned any hope of provoking him to some product worthy of his powers, and contented himself with the service that Alcott provided him. "Alcott is a certain fluid in which men of a certain spirit can easily expand themselves & swim at large, they who elsewhere found themselves confined. He gives them nothing but themselves. Me he has served now these twelve years in that way; he was the reasonable creature to speak to, that I wanted."[30] When asked "concerning Alcott's wisdom," Emerson had "not books to open, no doctrines to impart, no sentences or sayings to repeat." Their conversations were nonetheless elevating. It was not so much what Alcott said, as the lofty position from which it was invariably uttered. Emerson spoke of him as a "lens" as well as a "fluid," and as "a beautiful susceptibility," estimating means and access rather than any truths to be garnered.[31]

Some men might need a worthy antagonist to rise to the heights of eloquence. This was the abolitionist's fighting stance, and Emerson thought Thoreau's conversation "military" in this way: he "requires a little sense of victory, a roll of the drums, to call his powers into full exercise."[32] But Alcott's muse fluttered and collapsed in the face of contradiction: he first tried to shrug off any such ice on his wings, and if opposition persisted, he folded them in silence. Sometimes it might seem as if his was just a subtler skirmishing in the "military" manner: "Let the other party say what he will, Alcott unerringly takes the highest moral ground & commands the other's position, & cannot be outgeneralled."[33] Since he refused to contend, Alcott's superior tone disarmed most combative talkers (just as "Candor" promised), and the result was to raise the discourse to a loftier plane. It was this habit of mind that Emerson valued in him; probably it was what others despised: "whilst he lives in his moral perception, his sympathies with the present company are not troublesome to him, never embarrass for a moment his perception. He is cool, bland, urbane, yet with his eye fixed on the highest fact." For Emerson these were enviable qualities, but other judges are likely to prefer the picture Emerson paints of himself: "With me it is not so. In all companies I sympathize too much. If they are ordinary & mean, I am. If the company were great I should soar: in all mere mortal parties, I take the contagion of their views & lose my own. I cannot outsee them, or correct, or raise them. As soon as they are gone, the muse returns."[34]

When all was said and done, however, the question uppermost in Emerson's mind was the same as that in Alcott's: when will the muse return? In what circumstances and on what terms may the spirit flow through *my* vessel? Thus each sought the other not in order to hear a voice or find a vocation, as did the abolitionists and other men identified with causes; nor were they evangelical, attempting to become a voice for others, as again Garrison and his followers had chosen. Once more we see how the transcendental emphases — on private modes of discourse, on spontaneity and inspiration, on the primacy of the inner man — cohered in their doctrine of eloquence. The excitement lay in the fulfillment of one's powers; the moment of ecstasy was in being touched by the muse. Speaker, audience, thought, were mere means. "I am made happy by a new thought," Emerson reported; "While this thought glitters newly before me, I think Wall Street nothing. I accurately record the thought, & think I have got it. After a few months, I come again to the record, & it seems a mere bit of glistering tin or tinsel, and no such world wisdom. In fact, the Universe had glowed with its eternal blaze, & I had chipped off this scale, through which its light shone, thinking this the diamond, & put it in my jewel box, & now it is nothing but a dead scale."[35] There was no diamond, only mining.

Like his older friends and neighbors, Henry Thoreau also believed in eloquence — even more passionately, though he spoke of it less often, as one is silent where the sacred texts are concerned. He too had his "jewel box," where he stored up mementos of his brushes with the universe. Where he differed from his friends was in his attitude toward spontaneity. Emerson said of Alcott, "when he writes, he babbles," but of Thoreau, "he is impracticable, and does not flow through his pen or (in any of our legitimate aqueducts) through his tongue."[36] Thus in spite of the aid of Emerson and Horace Greeley, Thoreau had trouble getting published. His early works especially were stiff and labored. He found public lecturing "foreign and irksome," though he usually took what rostrums were offered.[37] Even tête-à-tête, his friends sometimes accused him of being incommunicative. Ellery Channing — who was himself notoriously moody and hard to get along with — complained that Thoreau committed his "thoughts to a diary even on [their] walks, instead of seeking to share them generously with a friend."[38] Thoreau's characteristic response was to transform the complaint itself into journal fodder: he swore, and dated it April 4, that he would throw away his pencil if he found himself guilty of such snobbery. The truth was that he always valued deliberate consciousness over spontaneous loquacity. Channing was not the first to find it a failing in him, or to be rebuked for telling him so. After Margaret Fuller pursed her lips at Thoreau's self-conscious prose — "the grating of tools on the mosaic"[39] — he waited his turn patiently, then retaliated in kind: "Miss Fuller's is a noble piece, rich extempore writing — talking with pen in hand — It is too good not to be better even. In writing conversation should be folded many times thick."[40] Better to err on the side of consciousness.

By the same token books were preferable to talks because the writer might choose his own mood, and that of the reader too — "a quiet and attentive reading mood. Such advantage has the writer over the talker."[41] In conversation, he admitted in his journal, "We are more anxious to speak than to be heard."[42] Friends became sounding boards. "An echo makes me enunciate distinctly — So the sympathy of a friend gives plainness and point to my speech. This is the advantage of letter writing."[43] His letters, Thoreau confessed to one correspondent, were chapters in a book of sermons, preached "to bare walls, that is to myself; and if you have chanced to come in and occupy a pew — do not think that my remarks are directed at you particularly, and so slam the seat in disgust. This discourse was written long before these exciting times."[44]

Thoreau seems to have had Emerson's response to company, and could be eloquent only when alone. Nor was Alcott of use to him in the way he was to Emerson. Unlike Emerson, however, he was apparently able to be alone even in company, and had raised consciousness to the pitch where correspondents and walking companions began to object. He wanted more than the "advantage" over them; he treated them as manikins, mere stand-ins for a wider, more deserving congregation. At times even his subjects — the much caressed facts of nature — can seem expendable, whatever the original cost of collecting them. The multiple revisions of his journal (at least before 1850) obliterated all trace of whatever was not a pretext for consciousness — as he himself dutifully noted: "I am startled when I consider how little I am actually concerned about the things I write in my journal."[45] The air is very thin at these heights, and it is a long climb from the "frankest speech, address most direct, proffered in meekness and love," that Alcott advocated as "the reformer's only weapon."

2. Speaking for a Cause

For the transcendentalists, to think about the uses of eloquence was to raise questions about one's relation to others. Propaganda or prophecy put one into tonal contact with an audience, and even the simplest exchanges with friends and acquaintances became problematic as soon as one had a truth to advance for action. Alcott was the first of the three to attach himself to practical causes. When Alcott came back from England in 1842 with his friends Charles Lane and Henry G. Wright, Emerson felt his old social anxieties redoubled: "I look with a sort of terror at my gate," he said in anticipation of their return.[46] There was a round of "conversations" — on the family, on property, on community — and Emerson found himself called upon to participate. "I came away from the company in better spirits than from any party this long time," he said grimly, "for I did not speak one word."[47] Another time he was not so lucky: "Today I have the feeling to a degree not experienced by me before, that discussions like that of yesterday and many the like in which I have participated, invade & injure me. I often have felt emptiness and restlessness & a sort of hatred of the human race after such prating by me & my fellows, but, never so seriously as now, that the absence from them is better for me than the taking an active part in them."[48] Later he reported, more laconically: "Yesterday English visitors, and I waited all day when they should go."[49] He particularly disliked the carping and denigration Lane and Alcott habitually practiced, keeping their moral sensibilities sharp — "not helpful, not rejoicing, not humble, not loving, not creative, — [so] that I said, Cursed is preaching, — the better it is, the worse. A preacher is a bully: I who have preached so much, — by the help of God will never preach more."[50]

If there were liabilities in speaking for a cause, even among friends, perhaps one could relinquish the speech while holding to the cause. It might be possible merely to live an exemplary life. "The true reformer initiates his labor in the precincts of private life," Alcott had said, "and makes it, not a set of measures, not an utterance, not a pledge, merely, but a life."[51] But just as Alcott could scarcely draw breath without talking, so for Emerson or Thoreau any living presupposed writing — and writing presumed a reader. Even in the woods, to live as "deliberately" as Thoreau purposed would involve continuously taking note, and that brought one up against the question, for whom? The most private awareness implied an audience, no matter how uninvited. As Ellery Channing and Harrison Blake discovered, Thoreau preferred hypothetical "neighbors," who might overhear his monitions without supposing that he was addressing them. *Walden* itself is full of this diffidence, at the same time that it insists on the universal urgency of its message — "to brag as lustily as chanticleer in the morning, standing on his roost, if only to wake my neighbors up."[52] It is hard to imagine a platform more removed from the ordinary purposes of public discourse, yet platform it is.

Alcott seemed to have had the least ambivalence about waking his neighbors up — perhaps because in his case there was so little danger of it. During the Fruitlands period, when he and Lane attempted to establish a utopian community that would rival Brook Farm and Hopedale, their voices became shrill and demagogic. Emerson called *them* "chanticleers," and complained about the "ruinous vice" the Fruitlanders had fallen into, of "gazetting" their every movement. "[A]s quickly as they have conceived a thing they are wretched until it is also published."[53] Self-conscious though it was, this crowing had not a trace of Thoreauvian irony to save it from the vulgarity of mere advertising.

This was Alcott's reformist phase, and Emerson's distaste for it was the same squeamishness that he felt with Garrison. As usual, the trouble with Alcott was that he could never be satisfied with *doing* something, but must also *talk* about it. There was, however, at least one remarkable incident in Alcott's later life that seemed to avoid most of the compromising entanglements of ordinary political discourse and presented itself as a symbolic action of the exemplary force that he was always seeking in his "orphic sayings." Thomas Wentworth Higginson, himself "reared on the antislavery platform," tells the story firsthand. The occasion was the first, according to Higginson, in which blood was shed as a result of the Fugitive Slave Act. A black man named Anthony Burns was in custody, due to be returned to slavery; a Boston mob, led by abolitionists of the militant wing, had already been repulsed by the marshals defending the courthouse. One deputy had been killed, but the besiegers' nerve was gone.

> Then followed one of the most picturesque incidents of the whole affair. In the silent pause that ensued there came quietly forth from the crowd the well-known form of Mr. Amos Bronson Alcott, the Transcendental philosopher. Ascending the lighted steps alone, he said tranquilly, turning to me and pointing forward, "Why are we not within?" "Because," was the rather impatient answer, "these people will not stand by us." He said not a word, but calmly walked up the steps, — he and his familiar cane. He paused again at the top, the centre of all eyes, within and without; a revolver sounded from within, but hit nobody; and finding himself wholly unsupported, he turned and retreated, but without hastening a step. It seemed to me that, under the circumstances, neither Plato nor Pythagoras could have done the thing better; and the whole scene brought vividly back the similar appearance of the Gray Champion in Hawthorne's tale.[54]

The extremely literary cast of the story must be credited to Higginson, whose predilection for quaint ironies was his failing as a social historian. There was no need to drag in Plato, Pythagoras, or "The Gray Champion." The event had its own drama. As Emerson exclaimed, "What a fact ... that when Higginson went to the Court-house having made up his mind that he should not return thence, the only man that followed him into it was Alcott!"[55] This is the irony worth exploring.

Alcott's own recollections of his motives in the Burns affair, put together twenty years after the event, read like a martyr's handbook: "I had an obscure instinct stirring within me that to die was about the best use that could be made of a freeman at that crisis, and felt that the wrong man had fallen on the wrong side. Had the victim been one of us, the sad fortunes of that day and of the country afterwards might have been less disastrous.... Moreover, I restrained myself with difficulty from rushing into the phalanx as it marched its prisoner down State Street, hoping thus to provoke a movement that might set the indignant citizens, standing on the pavements and watching the spectacle, upon the bayonetted platoons, and rescue the slave from being returned to his doom."[56] Alcott was seventy-four when he wrote this, and had forgotten much — had even misremembered the fugitive's name (he confused the Sims case of a few years earlier with that of Burns) and collapsed two separate stages of his experience (the rush on the courthouse and the march through the streets, days later) into one. Nonetheless, the motives ring true, and answer well his own call for "address most direct, proffered in meekness and love," as "the reformer's only weapon." He acted as he wrote, with a magnificence of cliché that only his utterly fearless abandonment of himself to the outcome could possibly redeem.

The greatest irony of all is that this, Alcott's most dramatic moment, should have been scarcely noticed in his journal for the day on which it actually occurred. His entire adventure was reported in a sentence: "I return by Court Square, where I meet Higginson and witness some incidents of the unsuccessful attempt at the rescue."[57] Odell Shepard conjectures that Alcott may have wished to avoid putting anything in writing.[58] Such an explanation would fit many other participants in the movement during those violent days, but Alcott was probably too innocent for such precautions — indeed, that innocence is probably the explanation of his own incredible performance, including his failure to memorialize it.

One by one the transcendentalists were lured out of their individualism into partisan statements and acts by the antislavery movement. Alcott, like Garrison, was a nonresistant — that is, a pacifist. In 1841 he had debated John and Henry Thoreau at the Concord Lyceum, taking the negative on the question, "Is it ever proper to offer forcible resistance?"[59] But the cutting edge of Alcott's nonresistance, like his abolitionism, had never been ground very sharp — there was too much Alcott and not enough Garrison, more oil than grit in the whetting. One suspects that he rather annoyed his abolitionist and nonresistant brother-in-law Samuel J. May, by telling him that slavery and war were "but branches" on the tree of evil, "whose root is selfishness, whose trunk is property, whose fruit is gold."[60] Sam May had been mobbed five times in a single month while organizing for the abolitionists, and cannot have been particularly receptive to these orphic pronouncements, especially since they were usually accompanied by a request for some of that "fruit" for Alcott's pure but bare table.

During the 1840s Alcott saw himself as a gadfly rather than an activist. He attended and discoursed at most of the radical conventions in Boston, but his mild blue eyes were more aware of the figure he cut than any doctrine he might support. His serious commitments were to "the homestead" — first to the utopian community he and his English coadjutor Charles Lane were trying to establish at Fruitlands, near Harvard, Massachusetts, and then, after its failure, to the acreage his friends and relations bought for him in Concord. If his fortunes had prospered, it is possible that he would have persisted in the style of country philosopher — "Orpheus at the plow" as Dr. Channing called him — but in the early 1850s times were worse than ever for the Alcotts, and Bronson confessed in his diary that he saw "A crisis of some sort coming, and to be met. No income, no earnings, etc. etc."[61] With the passage of the Fugitive Slave Act, the country seemed at its crisis too, and Alcott took the occasion to propose himself as traveling agent for the abolitionists, as his brother-in-law had dangerously served years before. What his motives were this time can only be guessed. In any case, he was turned down, as Thoreau reports, because he would not "train well *under*" Garrison and company — no doubt as true as it was galling a reason.[62] A few months later he volunteered to patrol the Boston streets as a member of the "vigilance committee" formed to protect "fugitives from being arrested during the night."[63] And in 1854 he made his solitary advance on the Boston courthouse.

The reactions of Emerson and Thoreau to the Fugitive Slave Act are more familiar than Alcott's. Emerson vowed "I will not obey it, by God," and he was among the first to see that the "filthy enactment" would make slavery an inescapable presence in the North, thus forcing the conscience of those who, like himself, had always had other causes closer to hand.[64] The theory was surely correct. Thoreau wrote "Slavery in Massachusetts" as his response to the Anthony Burns affair, and all three — Emerson, Thoreau, and Alcott — ended by supporting John Brown's more violent arguments in Kansas and Missouri.

These reactive statements, whether in the simple call of Alcott, "Why are we not within?" or the oath of disobedience of Emerson, or the more elaborate sarcasms of Thoreau, are all interesting examples of political language. But there is something forced, as Emerson had predicted, about them. The limits of rational discourse had been transgressed — the Fugitive Slave Act was made, Emerson told himself in disbelief, "by people who could read and write." These were not the occasions or terms on which the transcendentalists would have chosen to speak. One can learn little about their political voices from listening to them at this crisis, when they seem merely to merge with the general stridency. It is more instructive to attend their approach to these limits, as each of them adjusted his stance to the less hysterical exigencies of the 1840s.

3. Nay-Saying

The most famous political encounter of transcendentalism was Thoreau's refusal of his tax bill in 1846, with its consequent night in jail, and the immortal explanation of his behavior in "Civil Disobedience." Here were Alcott's exemplary act, Emer-

son's vow of disobedience, and Thoreau's own ironic afterword
— all in a single organic episode.

Not everyone considered the act exemplary. Emerson had
not yet warmed to his abolitionist fervor of 1851, and his initial
response to his friend's protest against slavery and the Mexican
War was less than enthusiastic. Shortly after Thoreau's release
Emerson wrote to his friend Elizabeth Hoar, who, since she was
visiting in New Haven, could not yet know about their neighbor's adventure. (There were those who thought that her father
"Squire" Hoar had paid Thoreau's tax to get him out of jail,
just as two years earlier he had kept him out of trouble when he
and young Edward Hoar had carelessly set fire to the Concord
woods.) Emerson begins facetiously, treating his letter as an
excuse "for counting up how many times I have been to Boston
since you were in Concord, how many hayrigging parties we
have made to the Whortleberry Pasture, and all other important
adventures." He continues in the same vein: "Mr. Channing has
returned, after spending 16 days in Rome; Mr. Thoreau has
spent a night in Concord jail on his refusal to pay his taxes; Mr.
Lane is in Concord endeavoring to sell his farm of 'Fruitlands';
Mr. E — but I spare you the rest of the weary history. It seems the
very counting of threads in a beggar's coat, to tell the chronicle of
nothings into which nevertheless thought & meaning & hope
contrive to intervene and it is out of this sad lint & rag fair that
the web of lasting life is woven."[65]

Frivolous as these sentences may appear, especially in the
light of the more serious reflections he was entering in his
journal, Emerson's account here is nonetheless instructive, for
it helps us chart the relative boiling points of transcendentalists
confronted with the brute facts of war and slavery. Only three
years earlier Thoreau himself had written a similarly jocular
report to Emerson of Alcott's archetypal encounter with the
friendly minion of the state, tax collector Sam Staples. His
paragraphs are worth comparing with Emerson's:

> I suppose they have told you how near Mr. Alcott went to
> the jail, but I can add a good anecdote to the rest. When

Staples came to collect Mrs. Ward's taxes, my sister Helen asked him what he thought Mr. Alcott meant, — what his idea was, — and he answered, "I vum, I believe it was nothing but principle, for I never heard a man talk honester."

There was a lecture on Peace by a Mr. Spear (ought he not be beaten into a ploughshare?), the same evening, and, as the gentlemen, Lane and Alcott, dined at our house while the matter was in suspense, — that is, while the constable was waiting for his receipt from the jailer, — we there settled it that we, that is, Lane and myself, perhaps should agitate the State while Winkelried lay in durance. But when, over the audience, I saw our hero's head moving in the free air of the Universalist church, my fire all went out, and the State was safe as far as I was concerned. But Lane, it seems, had cogitated and even written on the matter, in the afternoon, and so, out of courtesy, taking his point of departure from the Spear-man's lecture, he drove gracefully *in medias res,* and gave the affair a very good setting out; but, to spoil all, our martyr very characteristically, but, as artists would say, in bad taste, brought up the rear with a "My Prisons," which made us forget Silvio Pellico himself.[66]

Some allowance, as always, must be made for Thoreau's habitual tone. After all, he did intend to join Lane in his denunciations at the lecture that night — "perhaps" — and no doubt he sympathized with the position that his friends had taken. On the other hand, he had clearly not yet reached the point when he too would march off to jail. We find Alcott in 1843, Thoreau in 1846, Emerson in 1851, each saying his "nay" to the state: "I will not obey it, by God."

It has become the habit with commentators on these events to regard Alcott's as the seminal act, somehow germinating and coming to flower in Thoreau's "Civil Disobedience" — Emerson figuring merely as a bemused botanist. But the chronology itself is not so orderly as I have made it seem (Thoreau in fact stopped paying his taxes the same year as Alcott and Lane did), and even if it were, it need not imply influence. Indeed, such a view does all three — and especially Thoreau and Emerson — considerable injustice, since it tends to put their acts of conscience in the light of mere faddish postures, taken with an eye to opinions of the moment. Whatever feelings of mutual support may have circulated among them, transcendentalists were self-reliant if nothing else.

Some neighbor — it could have been either Thoreau or Alcott but it sounds more like Alcott — told Emerson in 1840 "that he had made up his mind to pay no more taxes for he had found that he owed nothing to the Government."[67] There is something rather blithe about this announcement. The play on words is Thoreauvian, but the sentiment has the studied nonchalance of Alcott's individualism. Let it stand, for the moment, as one extreme of the attitude toward taxes. At the opposite end of the spectrum we may place Squire Hoar, "the very personification of the State" as Charles Lane once characterized him.[68] Not only did the Squire pay, unasked, the taxes of Alcott and (conceivably) Thoreau — while his son Rockwood Hoar paid Lane's — but he once told Emerson, apropos of "some inequality of taxes in the town," that "it was his practice to pay whatever was demanded; for, though he might think the taxation large and very unequally proportioned, yet he thought the money might as well go in this way as in any other."[69] This generous cynicism, a principled disregard for principle, is a good match for the cavalier anarchism of Emerson's unidentified neighbor. The choice between them seems pretty obviously a matter of simple economic prudence, wealth insuring its goods, poverty tightening its belt. But there was more political and social philosophy lurking in these positions than might first appear in their casual guise as Emersonian hearsay.

In Thoreau's tickled synopsis of Alcott's taxation, he mentions that Charles Lane "had cogitated and even written on the matter," before the issue was known. Lane himself had also decided to pay no taxes, and one assumes their decisions must have been concerted, an emblem perhaps of their proposed withdrawal from society and venture into a new community of the regenerate at Fruitlands. In any case, Lane had thought about the question long enough to provide material for more than a mere impromptu harangue after a pacifist lecture. He wrote it up in installments, as letters to Garrison's abolitionist and nonresistant newspaper, *The Liberator*. The first letter contained the announcement and interpretation of the event itself. According to Lane, Alcott's act was "founded on the moral instinct which forbids every moral being to be a party, either actively or permissively, to the destructive principles of power and might over peace and love." Vaporous as this explanation may seem, it was probably understood by readers of *The Liberator*, who would have agreed that it was "tyrannous" for "the human will . . . to be subject to the brute force which the majority may set up."[70] Alcott's refusal of his tax was an "act of non-resistance."

"Non-resistance" was the name of the movement that had split the American pacifists in 1838, between the radicals led by Garrison and Henry Clarke Wright, and the conservatives in the tradition of William Ladd. While the latter had emphasized the need for nations to join together in some world federation, the nonresistants believed in more immediate and direct action. Since no existing government seemed likely to reform itself as completely as the radicals required — that is, the abandonment of all use of force, including that of police and tax officers — the New England Non-resistance Society advised noncooperation with the state in all its functions. Many became no-government men as well as nonresistants and abolitionists, and they saw their positions on these issues as mutually entailed. When Lane called Alcott's an "act of non-resistance," he meant, in modern terms, that it was pacifist, nonviolent, and anarchist — as we would say, "libertarian." Chief of these motives in the actual event was the anarchist, and the ensuing series of letter-articles that Lane wrote for *The Liberator* was called "Voluntary Political Government," an argument against most of the means and many of the functions of the state, which were to be transformed by making everything optional. Roads would be paved by those who wanted to use them, education would be the primary responsibility of the family (as Lane's hero Pestalozzi had said it ought to be anyway), each township would handle its own criminals and insane. Essentially, the locus of social responsibility would be shifted away from governmental bodies entirely to more natural and organic units like the neighborhood and the family. Lane and Alcott called their principle of organization at Fruitlands "the consociate family," and it was to figure as model for a world without the state and all its evils.

Although Alcott himself did not say why he refused his taxes in 1843, he did write quite a bit in his journal about taxes and the state in 1846 and 1847, around the time of Thoreau's brush with Sam Staples. It is interesting to see how much of Lane's programmatic vision remained with Alcott after the failure of their community. Here for example, in February of 1847, he sounds very much like Emerson's neighbor of 1840, who "owed nothing to the Government": "The State is man's pantry, at best, and filled at an immense cost — a spoliation of the human commonwealth. Let it go. Heroes will live on nuts, and freemen sun themselves under the clefts of the rocks, sooner than sell their liberty for the pottage of slavery. We few honest neighbours can help each other; and if the State desires any favours of us we will take the matter into consideration and, at a proper time, give them a respectful answer."[71] One might have expected Alcott to have taken a somewhat harder line, in reaction to the Mexican War and its resultant extension of slavery into Texas. These, of course, were among the reasons Thoreau gave for refusing his taxes the preceding year. Alcott too had considered withholding his in 1846, but his motives were unchanged from those reported by Lane in 1843:

> Staples, the town collector, called to assure me that he should next week advertize my land to pay for the tax, unless

49

it was paid before that time. Land for land, man for man. I would, were it possible, know nothing of this economy called "the State," but it will force itself upon the freedom of the free-born and the wisest bearing is to over-bear it, let it have its own way, the private person never going out of his way to meet it. It shall put its hand into a person's pocket if it will, but I shall not put mine there on its behalf.[72]

Much as this sounds like a decision to refuse to pay, in fact Alcott's land was not in his name at all, but in trust for his wife, and he knew that his taxes would be paid for him, if not by Squire Hoar again, then by those relatives of Mrs. Alcott who also supported him in other ways. What is significant is not the refusal but the manner of it. This may be regarded as merely a further extension of nonresistance — ignoring the state if one cannot quite defy it. "Resist not evil" is taken to include the state as well as ordinary thieves and murderers.

When Alcott and Emerson discussed Thoreau's tax refusal not long after, Alcott viewed his friend's act as he would his own. "E[merson] thought it mean and skulking, and in bad taste. I defended it on the grounds of a dignified non-compliance with the injunction of civil powers."[73] For Alcott, the injustice lay chiefly in the state's treatment of the individual taxpayer, less in the evils of slavery and war perpetrated on others.

Here again we may survey the range of civic obligations felt by the transcendentalists. In December Alcott told a convention of the Non-resistance Society that citizens could "rightfully refuse" to pay for the Mexican War, but his aim was not the end of that war so much as "a laying of the foundations of a new commonwealth, based on a catholicism commensurate with the needs of mankind."[74] Thoreau seemed to have his eye on the invasion of Mexico and the plight of the oppressed. "Under a government which imprisons any unjustly, the true place for a just man is also a prison. . . . It is there that the fugitive slave, and the Mexican prisoner on parole, and the Indian come to plead the wrongs of his race, should find them. . . ."[75] This was not a non-resistant position. Thoreau had never been a pacifist, and in that 1841 debate at the Concord Lyceum it had been Henry and his brother upholding the affirmative of "Is it ever proper to offer forcible resistance?" He took special pains in "Civil Disobedience" to distinguish his position from Alcott's anarchism as well as his pacifism; "unlike those who call themselves no-government men, I ask for, not at once no government, but *at once* a better government."[76] Indeed, the first title of the essay, when it was published in Elizabeth Peabody's short-lived journal *Æsthetic Papers*, was "Resistance to Civil Government" — verbally, at least, almost the opposite of the stance that Alcott had taken in 1846 when he resigned himself to letting the state rob him of his taxes.

In spite of these distinctions, Alcott very much approved of Thoreau's act, and he apparently went twice in 1848 to hear the resulting lecture, then called "The Rights & Duties of the Individual in relation to Government." The issue of resistance and nonresistance was not yet forced in the title, and Alcott seemed happy enough to see the Mexican War and slavery receive a good deal of attention, so long as his own protest in 1843 was also mentioned: "His allusions to the Mexican War, to Mr. Hoar's expulsion from Carolina, his own imprisonment in Concord Jail for refusal to pay his tax, Mr. Hoar's payment of mine when taken to prison for a similar refusal, were all pertinent, well considered, and reasoned. I took great pleasure in this deed of Thoreau's."[77]

When Thoreau finally came to publish the lecture under the new title, he excised his allusions to Alcott's precedence over him and, while retaining the reference to Samuel Hoar's expulsion from South Carolina as a Northern agitator, he failed to mention the Squire's payment of the taxes of Alcott, merely noting that in his own case "some one interfered."[78] It would have been awkward for Thoreau to ignore Alcott's "similar refusal" in a speech delivered before a Concord audience. Presumably many of their neighbors would know what Thoreau states in his essay without comment, that he himself had not paid taxes for "six years," that is, not since the time Alcott and Lane were arrested for not paying theirs. Whether Thoreau acted in concert with the Fruitlanders, or in response to their gesture, cannot be finally settled. The tone of his remarks on Alcott's exploit suggests a later commitment, perhaps the following year. According to Lane, Alcott had not paid his for several years before his arrest — another bit of evidence that he was the "neighbor" who in 1840 told Emerson he would pay no more taxes. In any case it must have seemed more in keeping with Thoreau's focus on the individual in "Civil Disobedience" to diminish those aspects of his position that might make it appear part of a movement.

Again, this is important because it helps distinguish the stands taken by the transcendentalists. Lane would figure as the extreme case here, with his emphasis on every feature of Alcott's tax refusal that suggested concert and community. Even his manner of broadcasting his views, in letters to the organ of nonresistance, Garrison's *Liberator*, shows a regard for tactics and propaganda that would not have occurred to Thoreau. Alcott falls somewhere in between Thoreau and Lane, eager for the golden age of "voluntary government" that Lane celebrated and that Fruitlands symbolized, yet still chiefly intent on his own single combat with the state. As Emerson said, "The fault of Alcott's community is that it has only room for one."[79] At bottom not one of them — Alcott, Lane, or Thoreau — could be called convivial, but surely the Timon of the three was Thoreau, whose interest in Mexico and slavery was, as he said, an anxiety to get off the "shoulders" of his fellowmen, so that he might go about his own business — to "wash his hands" of humanity's dirt.[80]

From a few hints so far, something of Emerson's stance on these questions may also be gathered. As usual there is a good bit of ambiguity to deal with. His attitude toward Alcott's "community" is ironic but not especially hostile, whereas his response to Thoreau's defiance of the state is full of annoyance — if we can take the words "mean and skulking" as literally his. Emerson's journal tends to substantiate Alcott's report.

At first Emerson appears to approve of Thoreau's act, as a protest against the Mexican War:

> Mr. Webster told them how much the war cost, that was his protest, but voted the war, & sends his son to it. They calculated rightly on Mr. Webster. My friend Mr. Thoreau has gone to jail rather than pay his tax. On him they could not calculate. The abolitionists denounce the war & give much time to it, but they pay the tax.[81]

Yet a few pages later Emerson's second thoughts seem to find Thoreau almost as much in the wrong as Webster himself:

> Don't run amuck against the world. Have a good case to try the question on. It is the part of a fanatic to fight out a revolution on the shape of a hat or surplice, on paedo-baptism or altar-rails or fish on Friday. As long as the state means you well, do not refuse your pistareen. You have a tottering cause: ninety parts of the pistareen it will spend for what you think also good: ten parts for mischief. You can not fight heartily for a fraction. But wait until you have a good difference to join issue upon. Thus Socrates was told he should not teach. "Please God, but I will." And he could die well for that. And Jesus had a cause. You will get one by & by. But now I have no sympathy.[82]

Emerson characteristically peers round every corner of motive and consequence. He must have known that Thoreau had stopped paying his tax about the time that Alcott had been arrested by Staples, several years earlier. Accordingly, the announced motives of the refusal, the Mexican War and the annexation of Texas, must have counted as rather after-the-fact in his eyes. Thoreau was spoiling for a fight, playing "the part of a fanatic to fight out a revolution on the shape of a hat or surplice." He had a grudge against the state, and was looking for some cause to use as a cudgel against it. In this he seemed to differ from Alcott, who simply waited for the state to request his taxes, and then refused on the ingenuous grounds that he did not want its services. Thoreau lay in ambush for the state, expecting it to overstep its bounds. One implication seems to be that Thoreau recognized legitimate as well as illegitimate functions of government. Another is that he was not quite candid in suggesting that he only wanted to mind his own business and had no philosophic axe to grind. Even granting the Mexican War as Thoreau's occasion for refusing his taxes, Emerson complained further "that refusing payment of the state tax does not reach the evil so nearly as many other methods within your reach. The state tax does not pay the Mexican War. Your coat, your sugar, your Latin & French & German book, your watch does. Yet these you do not stick at buying." This is mere byplay, however, since Emerson was convinced that Thoreau had other motives. "The abolitionists ought to resist & go to prison in multitudes on their known & described disagreements from the state. They know where the shoe pinches; have told it a thousand times; are hot headed partialists. I should heartily applaud them; it is in their system.... But not so for you generalizers. You are not citizens.... Reserve yourself for your own work." At this point Alcott is dragged into the dock too:

> A.B.A. thought he could find as good a ground for quarrel in the state tax as Socrates did in the Edict of the Judges. Then I say, Be Consistent, & never more put an apple or a kernel of corn into your mouth. Would you feed the devil? Say boldly "There is a sword sharp enough to cut sheer between flesh & spirit, & I will use it, & not any longer belong to this double faced equivocating mixed Jesuitical universe."
>
> . . .
>
> The Abolitionists should resist because they are literalists; they know exactly what they object to, & there is a government possible which will content them. Remove a few specified grievances, & this present commonwealth will suit them. They are the new Puritans, & as easily satisfied. But you, nothing will content. No government short of a monarchy consisting of one king & one subject, will appease you. Your objection then to the state of Massachusetts is deceptive. Your true quarrel is with the state of Man.[83]

It is difficult to separate the antagonists here — and in the long run perhaps it is unnecessary. We can hear echoes of the epigram on Alcott's "community of one," written only a few months earlier, but the "you" addressed must at least include the "you" chastised elsewhere in these observations, that is, Thoreau. His choice of going to jail rather than paying his taxes is equated with Alcott's dissatisfaction with the universe. "This prison," Emerson concludes, "is one step to suicide."

Whatever hard words Emerson had for Thoreau in 1846, by the time his crime had been turned into a lecture Emerson was softening the criticism. Typical of his growing ambivalence is an anecdote from his trip to England not long after, recounted in *English Traits*. The occasion was "a very rainy day," when Carlyle and Arthur Helps asked "whether there were any Americans? — any with an American idea, — any theory of the right future of that country?"

> Thus challenged, I bethought myself neither of caucuses nor congress, neither of presidents nor of cabinet-ministers, nor of such as would make of America another Europe. I thought only of the simplest and purest minds; I said, "Certainly yes; — but those who hold it are fanatics of a dream which I should hardly care to relate to your English ears, to which it might be only ridiculous, — and yet it is the only true." So I opened the dogma of no-government and non-resistance, and anticipated the objections and the fun, and procured a kind of hearing for it. I said, it is true that I have never seen in any country a man of sufficient valor to stand for this truth, and yet it is plain to me that no less valor than this can command my respect. I can easily see the bankruptcy of the vulgar musket-worship, — though great men be musket-worshippers; — and 't is certain as God liveth, the gun that does not need another gun, the law of love and justice alone, can effect a clean revolution. I fancied that one or two of my anecdotes made some impression on Carlyle.[84]

It is hard to imagine a sterner test of Emerson's best hopes for America than the question put to him, as a representative

55

voice, by these formidable Englishmen. All this preface and apology for "the law of love and justice" suggests that he was more than a little intimidated by his company and their question, defensive about his country and its "purest minds," who resist its laws and taxes. In his anticipation of "objections and fun" he is uncomfortable rather than gleeful, and the edging back and forth between seriousness and embarrassed cynicism provides a guide to his own problems of belief in the doctrines of his friends. Yet his answer, whatever its tonalities, nonetheless names nonresistance and no-government as the American contributions to the history of the race. That surely is a significant footnote to his journal of 1846.

In Emerson's journal, the interest in nonresistance went back a long way. In 1831 he was wishing that "the Christian principle, the *ultra* principle of nonresistance and returning good for ill might be tried fairly." Nor was he apologetic in 1844, when he published his essay on "Politics":

> The tendencies of the times favor the idea of self-government, and leave the individual, for all code, to the rewards and penalties of his own constitution; which work with more energy than we believe whilst we depend on artificial restraints. The movement in this direction has been very marked in modern history. . . . The power of love, as a basis of a State, has never been tried. We must not imagine that all things are lapsing into confusion if every tender protestant be not compelled to bear his part in certain social conventions; nor doubt that roads can be built, letters carried, and the fruit of labor secured, when the government of force is at an end.[85]

Why this expectant vision should have given way to the annoyed reasonings of 1846 and the embarrassed defenses of 1848, it is difficult to say. In 1844 he could not "call to mind a single human being who has steadily denied the authority of the laws, on the simple ground of his own moral nature."[86] Apparently neither Thoreau's nor Alcott's individualist stand gave him the example of "valor" and "truth" he awaited, for the same messianic expectation is reaffirmed in *English Traits* — rather compulsively and fainter by half, but still the hope America gives rise to, scarcely a dozen years before the Civil War.

Then, to complicate matters still more, in 1849 Emerson agreed to the printing of his own major defense of the doctrine of nonresistance in its pacifist bearings, a lecture entitled "War" that he had delivered under the auspices of the American Peace Society in 1838. That was the year that the New England Non-resistance Society split off from the Peace Society. Garrison, who was engineering the schism, made a point of praising Emerson's speech to Alcott, as well he might. The argument came out mildly but clearly for the nonresistant position, and paid only the most polite lip service to the Congress-of-Nations projects of the conservative elements in the Peace Society. That Emerson agreed to the printing of the essay in 1849, given the European context of war and revolution, is much; that it appeared in Elizabeth Peabody's *Æsthetic Papers*, along with Thoreau's "Resistance to Civil Government," is a great deal more. Of course he must have known that Miss Peabody was printing Henry's essay along with his, and that the two would be considered as mutually reinforcing. How could a sentence like the following not apply to Thoreau? "The man of principle, that is, the man who, without any flourish of trumpets, titles of lordship, or train of guards, without any notice of his action abroad, expecting none, takes in solitude the right step uniformly, on his private choice, and disdaining consequences, — does not yield, in my imagination, to any man."[87] Or again, remembering the accusation lodged in his journal that "No government short of a monarchy consisting of one king & one subject, will appease you," how does this sound?

> . . . a man should be himself responsible, with goods, health, and life, for his behavior; . . . should not ask of the State, protection; should ask nothing of the State; should be him-

self a kingdom and a state; fearing no man; quite willing to use the opportunities and advantages that good government throw[s] in his way, but nothing daunted, and not really the poorer if government, law and order went by the board; because in himself reside infinite resources; because he is sure of himself, and never needs to ask another what in any crisis it beho[o]ves him to do.[88]

Few if any readers would be able to compare these opinions with Emerson's journal, but surely everyone would see the resemblance to a passage in "Resistance to Civil Government":

For my own part, I should not like to think that I ever rely on the protection of the State. But, if I deny the authority of the State when it presents its tax-bill, it will soon take and waste all my property, and so harass me and my children without end. This is hard. This makes it impossible for a man to live honestly and at the same time comfortably in outward respects. It will not be worth the while to accumulate property that would be sure to go again. You must hire or squat somewhere, and raise but a small crop, and eat that soon. You must live within yourself, and depend upon yourself, always tucked up and ready for a start, and not have many affairs.[89]

Thoreau pretends, for rhetorical purposes, to find such conditions "hard," but the evidence of *Walden* all goes to show that "squatting," "raising but a small crop," and "living within yourself" were his preferences. These are the virtues of self-reliance, and so it is appropriate that Emerson praise "the man of principle," "disdaining consequences"; but Thoreau had actually chosen and enjoyed both the principles and their consequences. It is as if Thoreau supplied the acts, Emerson the theory and the appreciation.

Yet, as we have already seen, Emerson was continually foretelling the appearance of this king and kingdom, without recognizing (or really desiring?) their advent. He agreed that "the less government we have the better," and argued that "the

State exists" only to "educate the wise man" — "with the appearance of the wise man the State expires. . . . The wise man is the State." But apparently the time was not yet, and Thoreau not the man.

> We live in a very low state of the world, and pay unwilling tribute to governments founded on force. There is not, among the most religious and instructed men of the most religious and civil nations, a reliance on the moral sentiment and a sufficient belief in the unity of things, to persuade them that society can be maintained without artificial restraints, as well as the solar system; or that the private citizen might be reasonable and a good neighbor, without the hint of a jail or a confiscation. What is strange too, there never was in any man sufficient faith in the power of rectitude to inspire him with the broad design of renovating the State on the principle of right and love. All those who have pretended this design have been partial reformers, and have admitted in some manner the supremacy of the bad State.[90]

Emerson made the point often enough; one supposes Thoreau heard it. In any case, it is likely that Thoreau had access to many of Emerson's criticisms, expectations, and denials before he sat down to turn his confrontation with the state into literature. Perhaps his decision to leave Alcott out of the published version reflects a desire, stimulated by Emerson's commentaries, to separate himself from the nonresistant movement in general and Alcott's special purist version of it in particular. He is not one of the no-government men, he explains at the outset, and then he tries to find a path between Alcott's anarchism and Emerson's pragmatism. "It is not a man's duty, as a matter of course, to devote himself to the eradication of any, even the most enormous wrong." That answered Alcott. Next, addressing Emerson, he goes on to say that it is his duty, "at least, to wash his hands of it."[91] But the abolitionists and nonresistants would have denied the first proposition, and Emerson had already questioned the possibility of approaching the second without compromise. Was Thoreau willing to give up his coat? his books? What accessory of existence could remain untainted in a nation one-sixth slave?

A few paragraphs later Thoreau has a more telling formulation, perhaps because it is less guarded: "I came into this world, not chiefly to make this a good place to live in, but to live in it, be it good or bad."[92] The virtue of this axiom is that it cuts both ways, answering both Alcott and Emerson. It is Thoreau's business neither to make the revolution nor to exhaust himself in conventional dissent. He too holds Emerson's opinion, that it is the particular duty of the abolitionists to withdraw their financial support as well as their moral assent from a government that fosters slavery and aggressive war: "if *one* HONEST man, in this State of Massachusetts, *ceasing to hold slaves*, were actually to withdraw from this copartnership, and be locked up in the county jail therefor, it would be the abolition of slavery in America."[93] But by making this point, he seems to separate himself and his responsibilities from the antislavery movement. So why *did* he go to jail? How was this "living" his own life?

In his journal Emerson had compared the state to "a poor good beast who means the best: it means friendly. A poor cow who does well by you, — do not grudge it its hay. It cannot eat bread as you can, let it have without grudge a little grass for its four stomachs. It will not stint to yield you milk from its teat. You who are a man walking cleanly on two feet will not pick a quarrel with a poor cow."[94] This put the question another way — not in terms of ethical responsibility, how to "live with yourself," but rather as a matter of tolerance and common sense, "live and let live." Thoreau had an answer for such arguments:

> I think sometimes, Why, this people mean well; they are only ignorant; they would do better if they knew how: why give your neighbors this pain to treat you as they are not inclined to? But I think, again, this is no reason why I should do as

they do, or permit others to suffer much greater pain of a different kind. Again, I sometimes say to myself, When many millions of men, without heat, without ill-will, without personal feeling of any kind, demand of you a few shillings only, without the possibility, such is their constitution, of retracting or altering their present demand, and without the possibility, on your side, of appeal to any other millions, why expose yourself to this overwhelming brute force? You do not resist cold and hunger, the winds and the waves, thus obstinately; you quietly submit to a thousand similar necessities. You do not put your head into the fire. But just in proportion as I regard this as not wholly a brute force, but partly a human force, and consider that I have relations to those millions as to so many millions of men, and not of mere brute or inanimate things, I see that appeal is possible, first and instantaneously, from them to the Maker of them, and, secondly, from them to themselves. But, if I put my head deliberately into the fire, there is no appeal to fire or to the Maker of fire, and I have only myself to blame. If I could convince myself that I have any right to be satisfied with men as they are, and to treat them accordingly, and not according, in some respects, to my requisitions and expectations of what they and I ought to be, then, like a good Mussulman and fatalist, I should endeavor to be satisfied with things as they are, and say it is the will of God. And, above all, there is this difference between resisting this and a purely brute or natural force, that I can resist this with some effect; but I cannot expect, like Orpheus, to change the nature of the rocks and trees and beasts.[95]

This is one of the strongest passages in "Civil Disobedience," because it grapples with the ambiguities of the subject — "this double faced equivocating mixed Jesuitical universe." The transformation of Emerson's "poor cow" into Thoreau's "brute force" is crucial. It allows the analysis of the state as "millions of men" — not simply a helpless well-meaning beast and yet not Alcott's thieving ruffian either. It also paves the way for that disclaimer, in the end, of any desire to "change the nature of the rocks and trees and beasts," that is, the universe. Who now is the most reasonable and acquiescent in the nature of things, Emerson or Thoreau?

4. Orpheus

The reference to Orpheus at the end of the paragraph draws attention to a theme already prominent in the essay and about to reappear significantly in its final pages, namely the discussion of orators and legislators — Webster and his ilk — whose voices ought to be raised against the evils of the state, but were not. "There are orators, politicians, and eloquent men, by the thousand; but the speaker has not yet opened his mouth to speak, who is capable of settling the much-vexed questions of the day." The problem is not a lack of great men, so much as a lack of any man willing to speak out. "We love eloquence for its own sake, and not for any truth which it may utter, or any heroism it may inspire."[96] It is almost as if we were listening to Emerson once again wondering where the "man of principle," "sufficient valor," and "truth" could be. Of course, the unexpressed sentiment — lurking in the shadows throughout this essay — is that Thoreau himself has now chosen to be the one voice, the Orpheus whose song will transfigure the universe. Nowhere is it claimed; but everywhere we find the insistence that someone should say what Thoreau himself is saying, do what he has done. Is not his the voice of conscience he appeals to, then, and he the "man more right than his neighbors" who thus "constitutes a majority of one"? This is as far as Thoreau goes. Any further, allow this egotism any nearer the surface, and one can imagine the sort of tonic Emerson would have administered. Like Socrates and Jesus, Thoreau must wait for his cause. But there is clearly a bid for immortality in many of these sentences, and Thoreau must have had hopes for this essay, even if he had little expectation that its immediate reverberations would go much beyond Concord. This becomes clear when we compare the equivalent aspirations in Alcott and Emerson.

Whatever its applicability to Thoreau, Orpheus is surely the appropriate symbol for Alcott's ambition: the desire to find words that would compel belief and regenerate the spirit — the "reformer's only weapon," that no one "can confront or withstand; their armor falls at once from their limbs." The author of the "Orphic Sayings," who hired himself out at day wages in his neighbors' fields, was surely delighted with William Ellery Channing's praise: "Orpheus at the plow is after my own heart. There he teaches a grand lesson, — more than most of us teach by the pen." Over the years Alcott's faith in the power of words shifted from writing, to speech, to act-as-speech. But it rarely faltered through these transformations. He ended wanting life itself to be a form of eloquence, his own life a handbook of eloquent gestures like that at the jail-house in 1843, or at the courthouse in 1854.

Emerson, on the other hand, apparently continued to believe that he might effect something through his lectures and essays alone — as in fact he did. Whatever his waverings over inspiration versus composure, he knew he had force in his pen, and he used it where he thought it might do good. The list of his writings criticizing slavery, war, and the state is double Alcott's and Thoreau's combined. Sure of an audience, and increasingly comfortable in his role as spokesman and sage, nonetheless Emerson could never quite rest easy in his success. The career of Garrison intrigued him because it was so like and yet so unlike his own. "He is a man in his place," Emerson noted, trying to account for his charisma. "He brings his whole history with him, wherever he goes, & there is no falsehood or patchwork, but sincerity & unity."[97] "Eloquence is a universal organ, valued because it costs the total integrity of a man to produce it."[98] Perhaps some of Emerson's unresolved ambivalence about the propriety of spontaneous discourse comes from a desire to fit such a description himself, and a fear that he did not. "Yes, but what avails it, if it be fatal to earnestness to know much?" he asked in his journal, apropos of the "platform."[99] Apparently a sage could not also be a prophet. Much as he complained of "partialism" and monomania in the reformers of his day, he envied their fervor. "Every great and commanding moment in the annals of the world is a triumph of some enthusiasm."[100] Such ecstasies of eloquence were not to be his. "I cannot hope to make any thorough lights into the caverns of the human consciousness. That were worth the ambition of angels! no! but only to make special, provincial, local lights? Yes, but we obey the impulse to affirm & affirm & neither you nor I know the value of what we say."[101]

Thoreau, initially as ambitious of public acceptance as his neighbors, was soon willing to trade fame for glory. But neither sage nor prophet was the role he had in mind. Even "Orpheus at the plow" did not content his imagination — he would settle for nothing less than an exiled god — Apollo in his year's bondage to Admetus. This recurrent Thoreauvian self-image has been explored by Perry Miller in his *Consciousness in Concord* where he shows how the myth suited Thoreau's curious ambivalence, his early resignation from "practical" success, combined with the highest ambition for some other kind of perfection. Miller quotes a letter Thoreau wrote as early as 1841, already containing just this mixture:

> I am as unfit for any practical purpose — I mean for the furtherance of the world's ends — as gossamer for ship-timber; and I, who am going to be a pencil-maker tomorrow, can sympathize with God Apollo, who served King Admetus for a while on earth. But I believe he found it for his advantage at last, — as I am sure I shall, though I shall hold the nobler part at least out of the service.[102]

"Orpheus at the plow" was a satisfying image for Alcott. Thoreau's Apollo is not easy in the service of Admetus. The service was constrained, and at best its advantages were hypothetical. As the years went by, and Thoreau developed more trades and talents to further "the world's ends," still without any prospect of an audience for his "nobler" achievements, the ambition and resignation remained the same, but the effort of maintaining both soured the metaphor. He had developed a stance that required his constant attention. Like Alcott, he wished his own life to be an example, and like Emerson, he wished to make his contribution through writing. His life therefore was to be dedicated to poetry, and Walden was to be transmuted into *Walden*. But such an enterprise was only possible under the most rigorous conditions.

> As I go through the fields, endeavoring to recover my tone and sanity and to perceive things truly and simply again, after having been perambulating the bounds of the town all the week, and dealing with the most commonplace and worldly-minded men, and emphatically *trivial* things, I feel as if I had committed suicide in a sense. I am again forcibly struck with the truth of the fable of Apollo serving King Admetus, its universal applicability. A fatal coarseness is the result of mixing in the trivial affairs of men. Though I have been associating even with the *select* men of this and the surrounding towns, I feel inexpressibly begrimed. My Pegasus has lost his wings; he has turned a reptile and gone on his belly. Such things are compatible only with a cheap and superficial life.
>
> The poet must keep himself unstained and aloof.[103]

Where Emerson regarded Thoreau's going to prison as a form of suicide, Thoreau thought coming out, at least in so far as it meant reentering "the trivial affairs of men," much more suicidal. The quarrel was over "the state of Man" — whether society was its essence, or its corrupting disease. Here is the deepest impulse behind Thoreau's "Resistance to Civil Government" — not so much a protest against injustice and oppression as a revulsion from "a cheap and superficial life." Alcott's "community of one" was a result of his egotism; Thoreau's was a function of fastidiousness. His objection to society was less a matter of politics or morality than of taste and art. He thought of his own life as a kind of heroic poem, and could not allow himself to stoop in his character, except as a god of poetry and imagination might, briefly, in fable.

Ironically enough, Thoreau's efforts to "keep himself unstained and aloof" ultimately resulted in a much more intimate contact with his posterity, and a much more lasting political influence than either Alcott or Emerson achieved. If the antisocial remove of Concord jail or Walden Pond seemed to thin much of the warmth out of Thoreau's voice, it also fostered, perhaps forced, a note that no other transcendentalist could produce. Apparently it was a pitch that could be maintained only in isolation. Whatever the conditions, it was something that would be heard above the din of many would-be prophets a century later.

"Huts Are Safe"

"Huts, huts are safe."
Emerson's *Journals*

1. Manual Labor

Writing to Margaret Fuller in 1840, Emerson told her that his ambitions for *The Dial* had expanded to more than "purely literary" topics. "I wish we might court some of the good fanatics and publish chapters on every head in the whole Art of Living. I am just now turning my pen to scribble & copy on the subjects of 'Labor,' 'Farm,' 'Reform,' 'Domestic Life,' etc."[1] Of Emerson's contributions to *The Dial*, "New England Reformers," "Chardon Street and Bible Conventions," "Fourierism and the Socialists," "English Reformers," and "Man the Reformer" took up these themes. He did not quite cover "every head in the whole Art of Living," but he reported copiously on the "fanaticisms" that interested him most.

A branch of social action that becomes especially attractive when other avenues seem tainted or aimless is the effort to create new institutions, alternative life-styles, a counterculture. During the 1840s many radicals were drawn into a widespread movement to establish pockets and colonies of a better life in the midst of the venal society of trade and politics that seemed to surround them. Of the ventures in community, Brook Farm (1841-47) was the most famous. America had already seen many utopias, some of them very successful and long-lived. Before the decade was out, over fifty more had been initiated, and Brook Farm was the beginning of this new wave.[2] George Ripley, founder of the community, was very anxious to have Emerson as a member, either active or merely subsidizing. Early in the planning stages he met with Emerson, Bronson Alcott, and Margaret Fuller to invite their comments and participation, and he followed up his presentation with a letter to Emerson in 1840 that emphasized those features of the proposal most likely to appeal to transcendentalist prejudices:

> Our objects, as you know, are to insure a more natural union between intellectual and manual labor than now exists; to combine the thinker and the worker, as far as possible, in the same individual; to guarantee the highest mental freedom, by providing all with labor, adapted to their tastes and talents, and securing to them the fruits of their industry; to do away with the necessity of menial services, by opening the benefits of education and the profits of labor to all; and thus to prepare a society of liberal, intelligent, and cultivated persons, whose relations with each other would permit a more simple and wholesome life, than can be led amidst the pressure of our competitive institutions.

> To accomplish these objects, we propose to take a small tract of land, which, under skillful husbandry, uniting the garden and the farm, will be adequate to the subsistence of the families, and to connect with this a school or college, in which the most complete instruction shall be given, from the first rudiments to the highest culture. Our farm would be a place for improving the race of men that lived on it; thought would preside over the operations of labor, and labor would contribute to the expansion of thought; we should have industry without drudgery, and true equality without its vulgarity.[3]

A few years later a new ideology was superimposed on these principles when the community became a Fourierist phalanx, but from beginning to end Brook Farm tried to bring together manual and intellectual labor, the farm and the university. In this advocacy Ripley and his associates were treading the heels of an educational movement in vogue during the preceding decade. There had been an official Society for Promoting Manual Labor complete with its own general agent, Theodore Weld, who later worked so hard for the abolitionists. Numerous schools and institutes, especially seminaries, had been founded or converted to the work/study system. The hoped-for advantages were not only physical and mental but also financial, and for some of its advocates, the movement had the self-supporting education of working-class youth as one of its objectives, an aim that persisted in Ripley's plan for "opening the benefits of education and the profits of labor to all."

Radical as they may seem, these ideas were initially founded not on a critique of society so much as on a theory of education. European educationists like Pestalozzi and von Fellenberg had developed it in an effort to reform the rigid and unnatural schools of the eighteenth century. Applied to American conditions, the democratic implications could take on alarming proportions. Robert Dale Owen, who had been in von Fellenberg's school, proposed a system of "state guardianship," for example, which would have largely removed working-class children from their parents' influence and completely subsidized their education. The idea frightened even the radicals, and the whole movement was on the wane by 1840. Brook Farm took over some of these earlier purposes and combined them with its communal aspirations.[4]

The evidence that remains leaves it unclear how seriously Emerson considered joining the community. Some of his private letters reporting the invitation fall into a bantering tone, though his formal declining was polite enough. Emerson's journals, both at the time and later, have little to say in favor of organized communal life. He had praise for neighborhoods, and for a time he took mild pleasure in fancying a kind of casual university of friends in Concord — but these groupings were based on natural attraction. The associationists, especially the Fourierists, were trying to "arrange a heap of shavings of steel *by hand* in the direction of their magnetic poles instead of thrusting a needle into the heap, and instantaneously they are magnets.[5]

Whatever his own preferences, Emerson was well-disposed toward the Brook Farmers, and one major premise of their experiment seems to have fascinated him; could an intellectual, like himself, profit by devoting some portion of his energy to physical labor — especially farming? (A corollary concern was the possibility of doing away with menial services — not the labor itself so much as the servants who had to perform it.) At one level Emerson's interest in the experiment of manual labor was quite personal. It probably had something to do with his age and his health, in an era when books were being written about *The Disorders of Literary Men* and the remedies for sedentary occupations.[6] Never robust, in early middle age Emerson was on the lookout for regular and healthy exercise that would not cut into his work too drastically.

A much more significant, though equally personal motive was the uneasiness he seems to have felt about the modest income he had inherited from his first wife. "I please myself," he wrote in his journal, "with the thought that my accidental freedom by means of a permanent income is nowise essential to my habits. . . ."[7] It is probably fortunate for us that this hypothesis was never put to the test. In any case, the need for justification really centered in the "habits" themselves, not the investments that supported them. Returning to the subject, he wrote, defensively, "You think it is because I have an income which exempts me from your day-labor, that I waste, (as you call it,) my time in sungazing & stargazing."[8] He went on to repeat his belief that he would "live just as I do now," with or without "my Twelve Hundred dollars a year," but that parenthetical gloss on the term "waste" betrays the self-accusation of a man who had already unearthed too many scruples for one respectable profession when he resigned his pulpit in 1832. This need to justify himself emerges still more explicitly in the context of his thoughts on manual labor: "I have a pen & learned eyes & acute ears, yet am ashamed before my wood chopper, my ploughman, & my cook, for they have some sort of self sufficiency. They can contrive without my aid to make a whole day — and whole year; but I depend on them, & have not earned by use a right to my fingers or toes."[9] For Emerson, these personal motives led right into a theory of the social benefits of universal manual labor.

"Man the Reformer," published in *The Dial* in the year of Brook Farm's inception, is Emerson's major statement of his thoughts on labor and the farm, and how they might enter into the reform of domestic life. He begins with a discussion of society from the point of view of a "young man entering life." "The ways of trade are grown selfish to the borders of theft, and supple to the borders (if not beyond the borders) of fraud. The employments of commerce are not intrinsically unfit for a man, or less genial to his faculties, but these are now in their general course so vitiated by derelictions and abuses at which all connive, that it requires more vigor and resources than can be expected of every young man, to right himself in them...." Emerson is careful to explain that the "commerce" he has in mind is not limited to a few corrupt tradesmen. "We are all implicated, of course, in this charge; it is only necessary to ask a few questions as to the progress of the articles of commerce from the fields where they grew, to our houses, to become aware that we eat and drink and wear perjury and fraud in a hundred commodities." From this complicity, he moves to the sense of powerlessness it nestles in. "The sins of our trade belong to no class, to no individual. One plucks, one distributes, one eats. Every body partakes, every body confesses, — with cap and knee volunteers his confession, yet none feels himself accountable. He did not create the abuse; he cannot alter it; what is he? an obscure private person who must get his bread." Faced with this massive anomie, what can the young man do but "take on him the harness of routine and obsequiousness. If not so minded, nothing is left him but to begin the world anew, as he does who puts the spade into the ground for food."[10]

2. Communal Experiments

None of this, accurate and heartfelt as it might be, constituted a radical analysis. Emerson's complaints were based on middle-class intellectual values, and his agrarian solutions had more of the self-sufficient yeoman than the militant populist impulse behind them. So far at least, or almost so far, the Brook Farmers would not have disagreed. Especially at the outset, before they decided to become the "model experiment" of American Fourierism, Brook Farm was as middle class in ideology as it was in personnel. The problem was how to make the middle class honest, and how to bring everyone into it. They too thought agriculture was the beginning of an answer. But they also thought — once Fourierists, they insisted — that not only the farming but also the social life of the farmers had to be newly organized to produce the results they wanted:

> We cannot believe that the selfishness, the cold-heartedness, the indifference to truth, the insane devotion to wealth, the fierce antagonisms, the painted hypocrisies, the inward weariness, discontent, apathy, which are everywhere characteristic of the present order of society, have any permanent basis in the nature of man; they are the poisonous weeds that a false system of culture has produced; change the system and you will see the riches of the soil; a golden fruitage will rejoice your eye; but persist in the mode, which the experience of a thousand years has proved defective, and you can anticipate no better results.[11]

Like Emerson, George Ripley had been a Unitarian minister, and some of the rhetoric here seems meant to echo in a hall, but a more immediate source of its tone is the propagandistic fervor that came to Brook Farm with Fourierism. Emerson, bringing in essentially the same indictment of society, seems coldly analytic compared with Ripley. The tar brush approach has a different aim: to eliminate all alternatives to the associationist revamping of the social order. "Change the system!" is the cry.

Although it is not quite fair, let me quote Emerson's account of this antidote to the system rather than Fourier's or Ripley's; it puts his own stance in high relief. "Society, concert, co-operation," he wrote in "Fourierism and the Socialists," "is the secret of the coming Paradise. By reason of the isolation of men at the present day, all work is drudgery. By concert, and the allowing each laborer to choose his own work, it becomes pleasure. . . . It takes 1680 men to make one Man, complete in all the faculties; that is, to be sure that you have got a good joiner, a good cook, a barber, a poet, a judge, an umbrella-maker, a mayor and aldermen, and so on. Your community should consist of 2000 persons, to prevent accidents of omission; and each community should take up 6000 acres of land. Now fancy the earth planted with fifties and hundreds of these phalanxes side by side, — what tillage, what architecture, what refectories, what dormitories, what reading rooms, what concerts, what lectures, what gardens, what baths!"[12]

Emerson published this in 1842, before Brook Farm had converted to Fourierism, and so the sarcasm was not meant for his friends in West Roxbury. Nonetheless, much of his analysis applied to their undertaking, even while it was still in the planning stages. After Ripley had proposed the "new Social Plans" at that October 1840 meeting with the Concord transcendentalists, Emerson reacted in his journal: "I wished to be convinced, to be thawed, to be made nobly mad by the kindlings before my eye of a new dawn of human piety. But this scheme was arithmetic & comfort: this was a hint borrowed from the Tremont House and U. S. Hotel; a rage in our poverty and politics to live rich and gentleman-like, an anchor to leeward against a change of weather; a prudent forecast on the probable issue of the great questions of pauperism & poverty. . . . I do not wish to remove from my present prison to a prison a little larger. I wish to break all prisons. I have not yet conquered my own house."[13]

When Emerson finally wrote a reply to Ripley's invitation to join Brook Farm, it took him two or three drafts to soften his skepticism to a polite refusal. He emphasized his own unsuitability for communal life and hinted at some reforms that he hoped to get underway, in his own "prison." "The principal particulars in which I wish to mend my domestic life are in acquiring habits of regular manual labor, and in ameliorating or abolishing in my house the condition of hired menial service."[14] In a letter to his brother William he added a third intention, no doubt in part a means to the other two, but also important in its own right, first as a grudging recognition of the truth in Ripley's communitarianism, and second as light on how far Emerson was willing to go in experimenting with modes of living. "Then," he wrote, "I am grown a little impatient of seeing the inequalities all around me, am a little of an agrarian at heart and wish sometimes that I had a smaller house or else that it sheltered more persons. So I think that next April we shall make an attempt to find house room for Mr. Alcott & his family under our roof."[15]

Such a proposal must have sent a shudder through William Emerson. Alcott's chronic incapacity to support his wife and children was the least of his Skimpolean dependencies, or so most people felt. Half seriously, Emerson thought he should "be maintained at the public cost," and preferred to assume the burden himself rather than see it taken over by "the county jail or poorhouse."[16] As it happened, the long-suffering Abigail Alcott vetoed this part of Emerson's scheme for self-help, and he had to shift his solicitude to a project that sent Alcott to visit his English disciples, Charles Lane, Henry G. Wright, and their enthusiastic friends, as a boost to his panting ego. The invitation to domicile with the Emersons was then issued to young Henry Thoreau, who accepted board and room, for which he was to "work with me in the garden & teach me to graft apples."[17] The communitarian flavor quickly faded, of course, when Thoreau was substituted for Alcott.

For the rest, Emerson's plan of "Liberty, Equality, & a common table, &c." involved getting the servants to take dinner with the family. The housemaid "Louisa accepted the plan with great kindness & readiness, but Lydia, the cook, firmly refused — A cook was never fit to come to table, &c. The next morning Waldo was sent to announce to Louisa that breakfast was ready but she had eaten already with Lydia & refuses to leave her alone."[18] So ended the most dramatic part of Emerson's experiments in ameliorating menial servitude. The communal ship foundered on class structure and split on the division of labor.

They did somewhat augment their family when Henry Thoreau moved in. If not quite common table, it was more than merely another plate for dinner. The arrangement seemed to succeed well enough. Both Emerson and Thoreau were jealous of their studies, to the point of being unable to tolerate company, even that of close friends, "for a longer time than one or two hours."[19] "Friends will be much apart; they will respect more each other's privacy than their communion. . . ."[20] For those two a fixed abode together was probably a saving of time and words over the friendly visits that had preceded it. This was a typical entry in Emerson's journal: "You may come — no matter how near in place, so that you have metes & bounds, instead of the confounding & chaos of visiting."[21] "I am made for chronic relations," he noted again, "not for moments, and am wretched with fine people who are only there for an hour."[22] Even so, there is a hint in Hawthorne's journals that Emerson and Thoreau sometimes grated on each other during this period; from a conversation with Emerson on the eve of Thoreau's departure, Hawthorne seems to have gathered that

Emerson had "suffered some inconveniency from his experience of Mr. Thoreau as an inmate. It may well be that such a sturdy and uncompromising person is fitter to meet occasionally in the open air, than to have as a permanent guest at table and fireside."[23] Whatever the inconvenience, when the household finally gave Henry up, to go as tutor to the son of William Emerson, on Staten Island, Emerson was careful to stipulate a private room for his friend "be it never so small — 6 feet by 6, — wherein to dream, write, & declaim alone. Henry has always had it, & always must."[24] Surely it is significant that their experiment in cohabitation should end on this note.

Meanwhile another experiment in communal life was beginning. Alcott had brought some of his English disciples back with him — Charles Lane and his young son William, and Henry G. Wright. A whole new round of utopian discussions was inaugurated, leading in 1843 to the purchase of a farm near Harvard, Massachusetts, and the establishment of the Fruitlands "consociate family." Again Emerson played the skeptic — this time less hesitatingly:

> I begged A. to paint out his project and he proceeded to say that there should be found a farm of a hundred acres in excellent condition with good buildings, a good orchard & grounds which admitted of being laid out with great beauty; and this should be purchased & given to them, in the first place. I replied, You ask too much. This is not solving the problem; there are hundreds of innocent young persons, whom, if you will thus stablish & endow & protect, will find it no hard matter to keep their innocency. And to see their tranquil household, after all this has been done for them, will in nowise instruct or strengthen me. But he will instruct & strengthen me, who, there where he is, unaided, in the midst of poverty, toil, & traffic, extricates himself from the corruptions of the same & builds on his land a house of peace & benefit, good customs, & free thoughts. But, replied A. how is this to be done, how can I do it who have a wife & family to maintain?"[25]

Emerson's answer was, if you have to ask, then you are not the man to do it. But this was no deterrent to Alcott. If he was not Emerson's "man [who] quite unexpectedly shows me that which I & all souls looked for," at least he was one who never let ordinary impossibilities stand in his way.

One of the English friends, Henry G. Wright, quickly defected into the arms of radical feminist Mary S. Gove[26] — something of a shock to Alcott's chaste sensibilities — but by June the other coadjutor Charles Lane had purchased the required farm and paid Alcott's Concord debts, and they were busy planting about eleven of their ninety acres, "4 acres in Maize, 1½ in Rye, 1½ in Oats, 1 Barley, 2 in Potatoes, nearly 1 in Beans, Peas, Melons, Squashes, etc."[27] Over the summer as many as sixteen persons worked on the farm, but most of these — including the principals — were "wanderers," as Lane termed one of them, the "Adamite" Samuel Bower.[28] Transient agrarianism has never harvested much of a crop, and so it proved at Fruitlands. However, it is a mistake to suppose that this failure explains the breakup of the community. In fact they got most of their harvest in, though much of it was moral rather than vegetable.[29] At Brook Farm agricultural reverses resulted in cutbacks and belt tightenings, reorganizations and retrenchments, because the community was based on financial commitments. There it made a difference whether the milk got sold in Boston or not. But at Fruitlands abstinence was a principle, not an expedient, and success or failure was to be measured in a spiritual harvest. "I had all the training these could yield," Alcott wrote in his journal a few years after his Fruitlands experiences, "and so this, their best ends, were not lost on me, if my countrymen failed of reaping the Benefits there sown for them."[30] The experiment was in the culture of man. As Lane proposed, "If we can aid the people in any way to let self be conquered we shall do something. Lust abounds and love is deserted. Lust of money, of food, of sexuality, of books, of music, of art — while Love demands the power devoted to those false ends."[31] These are not socioeconomic motives.

When Alcott and Lane visited Brook Farm that summer, they found "80 or 90 persons playing away their youth and day time in a miserably joyous frivolous manner."[32] Not so at Fruitlands where Abigail Alcott memorialized a Sunday in July in her diary: "Mr. Alcott most beautifully and forcibly illustrated on the black board the sacrifices and utter subjection of the body to the Soul, showing the † on which the lusts of the flesh are to be sacrificed. Renunciation is the law; devotion to God's will the Gospel. The latter makes the former easy, sometimes delightful."[33] A few days later Isaac Hecker, who had defected from Brook Farm, recorded a typical Fruitlands after-breakfast conversation, on "the Highest Aim": "Mr. Alcott said it was Integrity; I, Harmonic being; Lane, Progressive being; Larned, Annihilation of self; Bower, Repulsion of the evil in us. Then there was a confession of the obstacles which prevent us from attaining the highest aim."[34] The Alcott children enjoyed similar entertainments. Sometimes Lane played his flute for them, and they studied music. Other childhood pleasures were equally edifying or productive. Louisa wrote one day in her diary: "Anna and I did the work. In the evening Mr. Lane asked us, 'What is man?' These were our answers: A human being; an animal with a mind; a creature; a body; a soul and a mind. After a long talk we went to bed very tired."[35]

Emerson seems to have lost interest in utopian communities after the first years of Brook Farm, for his remarks on Fruitlands are scanty in comparison. Perhaps he did not fully appreciate the difference between experiments, the one in "labor," the other in "love." Lane thought him "quite stationary; he is off the Railroad of progress, and merely an elegant kindly observer of all who pass onwards, and notes down their aspect while they remain in sight; of course when they arrive at a new station they are gone from and for him."[36] The skepticism was mutual. When Emerson came with Ellery Channing to see Fruitlands, he withheld judgment on their apparent "progress": "They look well in July. We will see them in December. . . . One can easily see that they have yet to settle several things. Their

80

saying that things are clear & they sane, does not make them
so."[37] But there is no mention, anywhere in Emerson's
observations, of the deeper significance of the moral experiment
being carried out at Fruitlands. He must have known what was
going on. A letter in early August expresses apprehension: "I
infer that no stability can be safely promised to the society; that
Mr. A. already anticipates the time when he shall be forsaken of
all, & left alone, inasmuch as none will probably stand by him in
the rigidness of his asceticism."[38] Then at the end of the summer
there is one further exclamation of foreboding inscribed in his
journal: "If our friends at Fruitlands should lose their
confidence in themselves —" nothing more.[39]

One suspects that Emerson did not want to know much
more than could be gathered from the surface. Brook Farm
had explored a theoretical problem for him, on which he
reported regularly — for example: "the experience of Brook
Farm was unanimous, 'We have no thoughts.'"[40] It confirmed
his growing suspicion of hard work. In May of 1841, when
Thoreau first came to live with him, Emerson was spending
"five or six hours a day in his garden and his health which was
in a very low state this spring improves day by day."[41] Well
enough, if all that was in the balance was effort and energy;
what about writing? "If I judge from my own experience I
should unsay all my fine things, I fear, concerning the manual
labor of literary men. . . . For, company, business, my own
household-chores untune & disqualify me for writing."[42] But at
Fruitlands it was not intellectual and manual labor in the test
tube, but lust and love. "Amelioration" was Emerson's carefully chosen word for his intentions regarding household economy, not "renunciation." Lane, in a letter to Oldham of 30
December 1842, reported that he avoided dinner time at the
Emersons; "a month of it, I think, would finish me, so I have
visited sparingly and always between meals." And this time no
one seems to have thought of inviting the Emersons to join the
"consociate family."

An invitation was issued to Henry Thoreau, however, whom Lane had taken a liking to. It is worth recording what Lane thought might be the "selling points" to a disposition like Thoreau's. His account of the beauties of the place began with apologies for his handwriting, hampered by blisters, and ended with these enticements: "For though to me our mode of life is luxurious in the highest degree, yet generally it seems to be thought that the setting aside of all impure diet, dirty habits, idle thoughts, and selfish feelings, is a course of self-denial, scarcely to be encountered or even thought of in such an alluring world as this in which we dwell."[43] Thoreau's reply is not preserved. At the time he was suffering from homesickness on Staten Island, and a return to his neighborhood would have been welcome. The temptations of simplicity and pure living probably would have added their appeal too, had they not been contingent on communal life. Although, as Alcott said of him, Thoreau was "coloring for half a dozen Socialisms," he was not available as a member of any organization.[44]

In other respects, however, Thoreau was an obvious prospect for the Fruitlands regimen. His combination of willfulness and self-denial, although turned to somewhat different ends, was enough like their own aggressive asceticism to intrigue types like Alcott and Lane. Isaac Hecker also tried to enlist him, for an itinerant commune of two, but with no better success. Thoreau seems to have had even less interest than Emerson in the outcome of such utopian enterprises. "Thoreau was in his own person a practical answer, almost a refutation, to the theories of the socialists," his friend noted. "He required no Phalanx, no Government, no society, almost no memory."[45] His private experiments encompassed the goals of both Brook Farm and Fruitlands — bringing together manual and intellectual labor on the one hand, and a pure and elevated spiritual life on the other. But results were hard enough to read without having to contend with other investigators and their variables. Thoreau wanted his answer formulated in units of consciousness. In the midst of all the talk about farms and labor and communities, he was noting in his journal, "I find incessant labor with the hands, which engrosses the attention also, the best method to remove palaver out of one's style."[46] While Emerson felt "exhilaration & health,"[47] and Alcott thought it was "good for me,"[48] Thoreau was perfecting sentences. Not many such would be written at Brook Farm or Fruitlands.

The experiment at Fruitlands turned out to be too stringent even for its principals. The tendency among students of Alcott to blame the failure of the community on Lane is as mistaken as the gossip that they were incompetent as farmers. Lane is supposed to have tried to talk Alcott into separation from his wife, perhaps even vows of chastity. A letter of Emerson's reports that Alcott and Lane had decided that "the Maternal instinct, & the Family . . . oppose the establishment of the community. . . ,"[49] but this must be seen in context. It was written in December 1843, at the very end of the experiment, when Mrs. Alcott's relatives had finally decided to bail her out of the prison of drudgery she was in. She had announced that she was taking the children and leaving. This finale must somehow be harmonized with Emerson's letter of 7 August already quoted, according to which Alcott "already anticipates the time when he shall be foresaken of all," the first of his self-fulfilling prophecies of the failure of his friends to live up to "the rigidness of his asceticism." Letters of both Alcott and Lane help fill out the story. In early August Alcott was discontent not only with his comrades but also with the Harvard farm, and was trying to raise five thousand dollars to buy what he thought was a better one at Leominster.[50] By the end of September Lane was complaining: "Mr. Alcott makes such high requirements of all persons that few are likely to stay, even of his own family, unless he can become more tolerant of defect."[51] A month later, ". . . all the persons who have joined us during the summer have from some cause or other quitted; they say in consequence of Mr. Alcott's despotic manner, which he interprets as their not being equal to the Spirit's demands." He also noted that Alcott had now decided against Leominster too, because it was not close enough to Boston — "the apprehension of being shut in here during the winter now that he has an impulse towards talking makes him rather impatient."[52] At this point Emerson was saying that neither Lane "nor my older friend give me any confidence that they will arrive at any thing in practice.[53]

There had been a still more serious falling out by late November, and it now clearly involved Mrs. Alcott as the defender of the nuclear family. Louisa recorded in her diary (20 November) that her father "asked us if *we* saw any reason for us to separate. Mother wanted to, she is so tired."[54] Lane had earlier praised "Mrs. Alcott's great energy,"[55] and his letter of invitation to Thoreau had described the burden of work as falling too heavily and unfairly upon her. In September he had worried that Alcott would drive his own family out of the community, and in October he said, "it should be stated that Mrs. Alcott has no spontaneous inclination towards a larger family than her own natural one; of spiritual ties she knows nothing though to keep all together she does and would go through a good deal of exterior and interior toil."[56]

Abigail Alcott had something to say about the matter herself. On 26 August she was lamenting in her diary: "A woman may perform the most disinterested duties. She may 'die daily' in the cause of truth and righteousness. She lives neglected, dies forgotten. But a man who never performed in his whole life one self-denying act, but who has accidental gifts of genius, is celebrated by his contemporaries, while his name and his works live on from age to age. He is crowned with laurel, while scarce a stone may tell where she lies." Probably she had Alcott or Lane in mind, though neither had exactly been crowned with laurel yet. She went on more pointedly: "A man passes a few years in self-denial and simple life, and he says 'Behold a God'."[57] This begins to sound like her version of the universal accusation during this period, that "Mr. Alcott is arbitrary or despotic."[58] After all, her acquaintance with Lane had not yet extended to "years."

By November Abigail's dissatisfaction had apparently overflowed her diary, and her complaints became a new problem for the community. Her lack of "spontaneous inclination" seems to have distressed Alcott as much as Lane, if we can trust the latter's account. "He one day spontaneously put this question to me — 'Can a man act continually for the universal end while he co-habits with a wife?'"[59] Lane asked the same question repeatedly in articles he wrote during the following year, but Alcott may have asked it first. Earlier in the month Alcott had been talking to Emerson about "marriage & the fury that would assail him who should lay his hand on that institution, for reform."[60] Thus Emerson could not have been very surprised in December when Lane told him that both he and Alcott were "wrong in all these years with Pestalozzi in lauding the Maternal instinct, & the Family, &c. These they now think are the very mischief. These are selfish & oppose the establishment of the community which stands on universal love."[61]

Whoever originated them, there is nothing very self-denying or "universal" in these bitter second-guesses by the consociates. Since Mrs. Alcott's decision was the axe to the project, it was tempting to blame her and to call her husband uxorious because he left with her at the final parting. It had taken Lane many months to come to the point of saying that Alcott was "borne down by his wife and family."[62] All the principals seem mutually estranged at this juncture, so it is not quite fair to single Lane out as the villain driving a wedge between husband and wife. His later relations seem at least as easy and friendly with Mrs. Alcott as with Alcott himself. One suspects that scholars have been misled by paying too much attention to Lane's own predilections as they later appeared in print — his attack on Brook Farm, his advocacy of celibacy, his joining the Shakers — none of which settles the question of his influence on the Alcotts.

Whatever the cause, by 26 November Mrs. Alcott had given "notice that she concedes to the wishes of her friends and shall withdraw to a house which they will provide for herself and her four children."[63] On the same day Alcott wrote his eleven-year-old daughter Anna, who was visiting those very "friends" in Boston: "All things remain as when you left us. But all manner of plans are drawn for our residence and way of living in the future."[64] In a month all had crawled off to lick their wounds, the Alcotts to "three rooms and use of kitchen for fifty cents per week" in nearby Still River,[65] the Lanes to the Shaker village across the valley.

Meanwhile by mid-November Henry Thoreau had fled Staten Island, thus cutting short his second experiment in "living in" as an adjunct to an Emerson family. Thus all three, Emerson, Alcott, and Thoreau, had had their modest taste of utopian life. Each now began to scratch in the dirt for a private nest — Emerson least anxiously since he had mixed for himself the smallest dose of communal fare.

3. Shacks and Summerhouses

One day, out on his favorite walk to Walden Pond, Emerson "met two or three men who told me they had come thither to sell & buy a field, on which they wished me to bid as a purchaser. As it was on the shore of the pond, & now for years I had a sort of daily occupancy in it, I bid on it, & bought it, eleven acres for $8.10 per acre."[66] The next day he bought an adjoining pine grove, and began to think of establishing Alcott on the land. His brother William remonstrated against any further financial gestures in Alcott's direction,[67] and for a second time Thoreau moved in where Alcott did not, since the land ultimately served as the site for his shack. Nonetheless, Emerson did not totally heed his brother's advice; within the year he had helped Abigail Alcott's relatives buy "The Hillside," eight acres and buildings near his own house in

Concord, as a "trust" in her name, out of Alcott's power to dissipate.[68] There Alcott rebounded from the Fruitlands defeat, in an ecstasy of compensatory husbandry — gardening, setting out trees, sodding, relocating barn and workshop, building arbor and summerhouse. Now began the "three years in private seclusion and communion with Nature" that he spoke of in his journal for 2 April 1848, the anniversary of his moving into "The Hillside."[69] Here in 1845 George Curtis remembered him "sublimely meditating impossible summer-houses in a little house on the Boston road."[70] At the same time Thoreau was clearing briars, getting out stumps, and generally improving his portion of Emerson's domain. He borrowed Alcott's axe to cut the timbers for his retreat, and bragged that he returned it sharper than he found it. Soon both had their homesteads tidy.

Towards the end of their first year of residence, their mutual benefactor wrote Carlyle about still another purchase he had made, forty additional acres on the Walden shore, where he proposed "to place a hut" that would rival Thoreau's: "perhaps it will have two stories & be a petty tower, looking out to Monadnoc & other New Hampshire Mountains. There I hope to go with book & pen when good hours come."[71] So Emerson, too, contemplated a woodland study. Indeed, the idea had crossed his mind when he bought his first Walden property,[72] but he could afford to see his friends quietly bestowed first, tucked away on corners of his land. After that, his own fantasies might be indulged. Thoreau offered a design for the hut, to which Alcott contributed the second story, "as a lookout."[73]

Although Emerson never built on the pond, he did not entirely abandon the project. Before he left for England in the fall of 1847, he hired Alcott to build him an elaborate summerhouse a few hundred feet from his back door, in what had been his cornfield. Again Thoreau aided in the enterprise, though this time Alcott was the architect and foreman, being more experienced in the trade since he had built both summerhouse and arbor during his first season at "The Hillside." Alcott's "mystic" architecture puzzled his townsfellows ("the strangest thing I ever saw"[74]) and amused his friends. Emerson threatened to call it "Tumbledown-Hall,"[75] but that was before it was finished. Lidian Emerson christened it "The Ruin" upon completion, and Emerson's son reported later that it was too draughty and mosquito-ridden ever to serve as the study it was intended for.[76] But it serves well enough as a final example of the curious fad among these Concord neighbors for hermitages and hideaways in woods and gardens.

What were these huts for? Emerson planned "to go with book & pen when good hours come"; according to his architect Alcott, "he hopes to ensure retirement and uninterrupted seclusion for writing."[77] Alcott's own arbor and summerhouse had a somewhat different purpose, determined by his self-image as thinker and conversationalist rather than writer. When Emerson paid him a call, he rhapsodized in his journal, "Worthy place, the arbour, for the reception of the poet as my guest. Happiest of men, to receive so happy a nature as this poet under a canopy made by my own hands."[78] On another occasion he reports this imaginary conversation under the same roof:

> "What are you doing, friend, there in your retreat?"
> "I am thinking."
> "Idler! Callest that 'doing'? Nothing comes, or can by any means come, of that nothingness."
> "Stay, friend. Thoughts are the parents of deeds. Now I am ambitious of begetting an illustrious family."[79]

Of course Thoreau had similar "private business" to transact in his shack. "I have a great deal of company in my house," he wrote, "especially in the morning, when nobody calls."[80]

The emphasis in both Emerson and Thoreau is put heavily on solitude, but it was not merely a matter of finding some peace and quiet for writing, as Alcott's slightly different case helps us see. Emerson admitted in his journal, "A scholar has no family: though he marry & keep house, there is yet no fireside in that house, but every one steals to his own room."[81] "A man thinking," Thoreau wrote, "is always alone, let him be where he will."[82] Society might be distracting to thought, but thought was fatal to society.

Not long after Thoreau went out to Walden Emerson wrote this in his notebook:

> Men go through the world each musing on a great fable dramatically pictured & rehearsed before him. If you speak to the man, he turns his eyes from his own scene, & slower or faster endeavors to comprehend what you say. When you have done speaking, he returns to his private music. Men generally attempt early in life to make their brothers first, afterwards their wives, acquainted with what is going forward in their private theatre, but they soon desist from the attempt on finding that they also have some farce or perhaps some ear- & heart-rending tragedy forward on their secret boards on which they are intent, and all parties acquiesce at last in a private box with the whole play performed before himself *solus*.[83]

Again there is a matching passage in *Walden*:

> By a conscious effort of the mind we can stand aloof from actions and their consequences; and all things, good and bad, go by us like a torrent. . . . I only know myself as a human entity; the scene, so to speak, of thoughts and affections; and am sensible of a certain doubleness by which I can stand as remote from myself as from another. However intense my experience, I am conscious of the presence and criticism of a part of me, which, as it were, is not a part of me, but spectator, sharing no experience, but taking note of it; and that is no more I than it is you. When the play, it may be the tragedy, of life is over, the spectator goes his way. It was a kind of fiction, a work of the imagination only, so far as he was concerned. This doubleness may easily make us poor neighbors and friends sometimes.[84]

Both these passages question the primacy of "actual experience," and suggest, with more or less satisfaction, that the life of the imagination may supersede reality. Thoreau affirms it the more strongly: "I find the actual to be far less real to me than the imagined. . . . Our thoughts are the epochs in our life: all else is but as a journal of the winds that blew while we were here."[85] Emerson's version is less assured. The double consciousness is fully embraced by Thoreau, while Emerson seems reluctant to acquiesce in the "private box." And in another passage he was even more explicit about his misgivings:

> The worst feature of our biography is that it is a sort of double consciousness, that the two lives of the Understanding & of the Soul which we lead, really show very little relation to each other, that they never meet & criticize each other, but one prevails now, all buzz & din, & the other prevails then, all infinitude & paradise, and with the progress of life the two discover no greater disposition to reconcile themselves.[86]

Much as he ultimately agreed with Thoreau, Emerson felt the tug of "the actual" more insistently. It is altogether appropriate that Thoreau should be the first to withdraw to the theater of the imagination at Walden, while Emerson merely commissioned a summerhouse in his cornfield.

Although part of the purpose of the hideaway in the woods was to discourage morning callers, its more important function was to provide the right setting for the play of the imagination. This is not merely a semantic distinction. Both are saying, Emerson with his allegory, Thoreau with his paradoxes, that the imagination will work on, whatever the circumstances. The theater in the woods was a symbolic recognition of the facts of imaginative life, as well as an attempt to force them. These transcendental huts represented an impulse to contract the energies into smaller compass, to draw a circle around the self and establish its grounds, to achieve what Emerson called "self-union" as well as "consciousness."[87] To move into a hut would be to enter into such a life completely. (Once there, of course, the goal receded. The imagination is not a place.)

This was the opposite of the communitarian drive to expand and branch out into every possible corner of social economy. Emerson had said earlier, when he was analyzing his reasons for not joining Brook Farm, "I should like to make my estate a document of my faith, and not an anomalous fact which was common to me, a believer, with a thousand unbelievers. I know there must be a possible property which flows directly from the nature of man, and which may be earned and expended in perfect consent with the growth of plants, the ebb and flow of tides, and the orbit of planets. . . . I only wish to make my house as simple as my vocation."[88] The buildings of a community represented its vocations and its imaginative life — a plan and a place for everything — while the hut stood for a single mind, a single imagination — perhaps, as Thoreau said of himself, with "as many trades as fingers,"[89] but all at the service of a single thought. "I do not wish to be any more busy with my hands than is necessary," he said in another passage. "My head is hands and feet. I feel all my best faculties concentrated in it."[90]

These considerations raise the questions of labor, vocation, and private property. Emerson had accused himself of being all "eyes" and "ears" and "pen," his dependency on others for manual labor depriving him of the "right to my fingers or toes."[91] Thoreau had opposite misgivings. He warned himself, several years before he actually went out to Walden:

> I must not lose any of my freedom by being a farmer and landholder. Most who enter on any profession are doomed men. The world might as well sing a dirge over them forthwith. The farmer's muscles are rigid. He can do one thing long, not many well. His pace seems determined henceforth; he never quickens it. A very rigid Nemesis is his fate. When the right wind blows or a star calls, I can leave this arable and grass ground, without making a will or settling my estate.[92]

There is a light in which Thoreau's entire career looks like an attempt to find ways of avoiding work. His often repeated conception of himself as Apollo in the service of King Admetus is part of this antipathy. "Men labor under a mistake" is a more famous formulation.[93] Whenever he writes in his journal about his plans to settle down in a shack somewhere, his thoughts seem to end on the subject of labor: "I only ask a clean seat. I will build my lodge on the southern slope of some hill, and take there the life the gods send me. Will it not be employment enough to accept gratefully all that is yielded me between sun and sun?"[94] Again: "I want to go soon and live away by the pond, where I shall hear only the wind whispering among the reeds. It will be a success if I shall have left myself behind. But my friends ask what I will do when I get there. Will it not be employment enough to watch the progress of the seasons?"[95] These were fantasies he toyed with in 1841, four years before he borrowed Alcott's axe and began building. By the time he had taken up occupancy, and along with it, his "employment," he had some further observations on the relations of living and getting a living, ultimately recorded in "Where I Lived, and What I Lived For." "There is some of the same fitness in a man's building his own house," he said, "that there is in a bird's building its own nest. Who knows but if men constructed their dwellings with their own hands, and provided food for themselves and families simply and honestly enough, the poetic faculty would be universally developed, as birds universally sing when they are so engaged?"[96] He followed this up with a new discussion of "employment," this time not attacking labor itself, but the division of labor:

> Shall we forever resign the pleasure of construction to the carpenter? What does architecture amount to in the experience of the mass of men? I never in all my walks came across a man engaged in so simple and natural an occupation as building his house. We belong to the community. It is not the tailor alone who is the ninth part of a man; it is as much the preacher, and the merchant, and the farmer. Where is this

division of labor to end? and what object does it finally serve? No doubt another *may* also think for me; but it is not therefore desirable that he should do so to the exclusion of my thinking for myself.

Although Thoreau included the farmer in his list of partial men, it was easy enough to see that the farm or homestead was the last citadel of the "whole man." He who built his own house, caught his own fish, and hoed his own beans, might also think for himself. The hitch was that the integrity of the self seemed to demand solitude, for the same reasons that the symbol of integrity, the hut, represented a life of isolation. In society there were too many complications and complicities. Emerson, for example, had encountered the resistance of his own family and dependents in his efforts at self-union. No matter how he might try to make the arrangements of his household "as simple as my vocation," there were encroachments and inevitabilities — Lydia refused to give up her role as cook, and Thoreau assumed the duties of gardener, thus pruning Emerson himself back into his study. In "Man the Reformer," he had formulated the universal dilemma behind his personal impasse: "I do not charge the merchant or the manufacturer. The sins of our trade belong to no class, to no individual. One plucks, one distributes, one eats. . . . That is the vice, — that no one feels himself called to act for man, but only as a fraction of man."[97] It was up to each man to assume the responsibility for his own actions and life, although the cost might be very great.

> Of course, whilst another man has no land, my title to mine, your title to yours, is at once vitiated. Inextricable seem to be the twinings and tendrils of this evil, and we all involve ourselves in it the deeper by forming connexions, by wives and children, by benefits and debts.
>
> It is considerations of this kind which have turned the attention of many philanthropic and intelligent persons to the claims of manual labor as part of the education of every

young man. If the accumulated wealth of the past genera-
tions is thus tainted, — no matter how much of it is offered to
us, — we must begin to consider if it were not the nobler part
to renounce it, and to put ourselves into primary relations
with the soil and nature, and abstaining from whatever is
dishonest and unclean, to take each of us bravely his part,
with his own hands, in the manual labor of the world.

But it is said, "What! will you give up the immense advantages reaped from the division of labor, and set every man to
make his own shoes, bureau, knife, wagon, sails, and needle?
This would be to put men back into barbarism by their own
act." I see no instant prospect of a virtuous revolution; yet I
confess, I should not be pained at a change which threatened
a loss of some of the luxuries or conveniencies of society, if it
proceeded from a preference of the agricultural life out of the
belief, that our primary duties as men could be better dis-
charged in that calling. Who could regret to see a high
conscience and a purer taste exercising a sensible effect on
young men in their choice of occupation, and thinning the
ranks of competition in the labors of commerce, of law, and
of state?[98]

Virtuous or not, this revolution would be hard to make. Even
in the consociate family at Fruitlands, where the effort to
maintain individual integrity was conscious, the inmates fell
into roles immediately, and the division of labor spread like
weeds through the garden. Lane recorded it: "Abraham is
ploughing, Larnard [Larned] bringing some turf about the
house, Alcott doing a thousand things, Bower and I have well
dug a sandy spot for carrots, the children and Lady are busy in
their respective ways, and some hirelings are assisting."[99] They
even brought in a carpenter to make bookshelves for the
library.

To be completely free of this dismemberment one had to
live alone like Thoreau. A member of a community, or even a
family, must divide and share the burdens of existence and thus
be only a "fraction of man." By this measuring, of course, the
summerhouses of Alcott and Emerson were seasonal at best,

gestures in the direction of Thoreau's independence. Nonetheless, the symbolic ramifications of their huts in the woods are far-reaching. If manual labor was the recommended therapy, it was equally clear that not just any hard work would do. The Irish "hands" on the railroad, or the Lowell mill "operatives," were alienated labor in their very names. The farm was the key to the integrity of labor, for there it was still possible to be independent of the rest of society. "You must hold the reins in your own hands, & not trust to your horse. The farm must be a system, a circle, or its economy is naught."[100]

However free of the division of labor and its evils, the independent agrarian did seem to depend on another suspicious institution — private property. The farmer needed a field, the homesteader a plot to build on. Even the hut designed merely for seclusion and study was necessarily private, and so entered the equation as property rather than labor. The "primary relations with the soil and nature" seemed to consist of owning as well as hoeing and harvesting. The division of labor occurred on a social plane, where rights of property were irrelevant, if not a positive hindrance; conversely, the self-sufficient individual, who wished to exist outside that realm, had to plant himself on the land, on private property.

4. Labor versus Property

These issues, the rival claims of property and labor, bring into focus the underlying conflict between Emerson, Thoreau, and Alcott on the one hand, and communitarians like the Brook Farmers on the other. Emerson stated the "doctrine of the farm": "that every man ought to stand in primary relations with the work of the world, ought to do it himself, and not to suffer the accident of his having a purse in his pocket, or his having been bred to some dishonorable and injurious craft, to sever him from those duties."[101] The Brook Farmers might seem to agree with this. After all, their original idea had been to unify rather than to diversify labor, so that each member could work with his hands as well as his head. But even before the institution of Fourier's series and orders by which they were finally organized into an "efficient" work force, there had been a helter-skelter division of labor, along lines of skills, inclinations, and most of all, sex. Women cooked, sewed, washed, ironed, swept, and so on. Men worked in fields or stables according to their talents. The future author of *The Blithedale Romance* shoveled manure, hoed potatoes, raked hay, but was not much of a hand at the subtler tasks. "I have milked a cow!" he boasted during his first week at the Farm,[102] but the experienced farmers William Allen and Frank Farley handled the livestock and plough and made all the important agricultural decisions. Even so, Hawthorne, who left after the first harvest, boasted to Emerson in 1843 that he had lived there "during its heroic age: then all were intimate & each knew well the other's work; priest & cook conversed at night of the day's work. Now they complain that they are separated & such intimacy can not be. — There are a hundred souls."[103]

Once Brook Farm converted to Fourierism, the division of labor became part of the official ideology. The Fourierist theory of the passions was an analysis of human nature to determine the laws of "attractive industry" — thus the famous assignment of garbage-collecting in the ideal phalanx to the young boys, who loved dirt anyway. "Harmony" was another key word, the perfect tuning of every talent to its use, so that large groups could live together, taking advantage of each other's proximity and skills to achieve what could never be accomplished in isolation, or even by the combined efforts of ordinary society's competitive and ill-regulated forces.

Charles Dana, one of the traveling spokesmen for the Brook Farm community, used to distinguish several stages of achievement: "Our ulterior aim is nothing less than Heaven on

Earth. . . . As the first step to this end, we advocate Industrial Association . . . ; the practical result we first aim at is Wealth . . . ; as this is attained, we shall see a development of [man's] social and spiritual nature which we do not now imagine."[104] The trouble with Dana's higher goals was not merely their unimaginableness. To a transcendentalist the means loomed large. As Emerson put it, "These are military minds, and . . . they have no other end than to make a tool of their companion."[105] "But lo!" said Thoreau, "men have become the tools of their tools."[106] In truth, this socialism was just a more lucrative form of capitalism, as Emerson was quick to point out. "The 'Community' of socialism is only the continuation of the same movement which made the joint stock companies for manufacturers, mining, insurance, banking, & the rest. It has turned out cheaper to make calico by companies, & it is proposed to bake bread & to roast mutton by companies, & it will be tried & done."[107] Brook Farm was itself a joint-stock company, "the payment of a fixed interest being guaranteed to the subscribers, and the subscription itself secured by the real estate."[108]

It was at this nexus — the relation of the division of labor to private ownership — that both theoretical and practical difficulties appeared. There was some question, as Emerson had suspected, of the loss of ordinary competence by relying on others for whatever was not a part of one's specialty. The problem might not come out in the "first" division of labor, but in the subdivisions after that. "The obvious objection to the indulgence of particular talent & refusing to be man of all work is the rapid tendency to farther subdivision & attenuation, until there shall be no manly man."[109] Nor was the distance that opened between production and consumption merely a matter of alienation, the slow drift towards the twentieth century. By making it possible to act at several removes from results, men had cut themselves off from responsibility. Blame was spread so thin as to coat all with uneasiness, but none so black as to acknowledge guilt — "every body confesses . . . yet none feels himself accountable."[110]

Yet the communitists were able to ignore these dangers of the division of labor, keeping their eyes on the game of suiting the individual to the job — a secularized and psychologized version of religious vocation — always played with the end of social wealth and harmony in view. The problem of private ownership was harder for the communitists to handle — for a very good reason. A neutral analysis might suggest that many forms of private property — especially the means and materials of production, land, natural resources, and the like — would necessarily become communal in any large-scale experiment with the division of labor. Whatever bureaucratic record might be kept, and whatever disproportionate dividends might be paid out on shares, the principle of association meant that all the social wealth had to be considered at once, when making decisions about its distribution and employment. Even if such decisions were not made democratically — though in the communities they usually were — the essence of the new "industrial order" was a recognition that the public good came first, before any private advantage. This was not primarily a doctrine of ethics or religion, but one of political economy, as the Fourierists hastened to explain. Thus they insisted on the distinction between associationism and what they called "communism" — a category embracing "those monotonous and monastic trials which have been attempted or executed by Mr. Owen, the Rappites, Shakers, and others,"[111] camps that did not mind admitting that there could be no true private property in a society that wished to take advantage of the power of concert, or order and plan for the common good.

The eagerness of the Fourierists to defend private property, incompatible though it was with their other principles, was taken by some as a sign of their fundamental kinship with the society they claimed to be renovating. This accusation is probably just, at least insofar as it calls into question the consistency of Fourierist theory, which for all its superficial mathematics was as confused and piecemeal as the rapidly changing economic context of trade and industry in the United

States. A clearer analysis (there were few to attempt it) puts the associationists somewhere just to the left of established society, on a spectrum that extended to Shaker communism at one extreme, and Thoreau's hut by Walden Pond at the other.

It would be easy to complicate and confuse these reference points; circumstance is no respecter of theory. But the anomalies can be accounted for, at no great cost to the simplicity of the analysis. Charles Lane, Alcott's comrade at Fruitlands, who had begun his career as a successful London businessman, came as close as any to a comprehensive, if partial view.

After the breakup of Fruitlands, Lane joined the Shakers for a time. When Emerson and Mrs. Alcott's relatives announced their intention of purchasing "The Hillside," Lane received an invitation from the Alcotts to live with them, in a new Fruitlands. In responding, Lane objected that Emerson's gift was not "wholly on universal grounds," but merely "an act of the purest individual friendship." It helps measure the distance between Lane's communitism and Emerson's individualism to know that Lane thought this mere friendship an insuperable hindrance. "I apprehend this basis will vitiate and mar, if not entirely neutralize, the good moral result that could not fail to arise in an old building founded on the true rock. It is no worse than the old world, but it is far behind Fruitlands or this [the Shakers'] work. My resolution would be to live in caves and log huts till we can build better dwellings. . . ."[112]

The great attraction of the Shakers, as Charles Lane saw it, was their purity of principle, the fact that they made none of the compromises that kept Emerson off "universal grounds." In "Social Tendencies," an article published in *The Dial* in 1843, Lane wrote on the alienation of modern man in almost Emersonian terms: "Every one looks abroad to every other one; no one looks within to himself; — a universal representative life, in which the legislator represents the conscience, the judge the gravity, the priest the piety, the doctor the learning, the mechanic the skill of the community; and no one person needs be conscientious, grave, pious, learned and skilful. Out of this grow those monstrous and dreadful conditions which large cities, the very acme of civilized life, without exception, exhibit."[113] His solution, however, was not Emerson's return to the farm, but rather a slow progress from the rational improvement of Fourierist "attractive industry" to the instinctive roles of the members of a Shaker family.

Brook Farm, although a step beyond "the present isolate competitive mode" of society, was not a true community in Lane's view. The Brook Farmers had seen that it was "impossible to introduce into separate families even one half of the economies, which the present state of science furnishes to man." But they were too cautious. Without total community of goods and persons, Brook Farm "is merely an aggregation," "lacks that oneness of spirit, which is probably needful to make it of deep and lasting value to mankind.[114] The Shakers had achieved what the Fourierists had only imagined. "'Attractive Industry and Moral Harmony,' on which Fourier dwells so promisingly, have long characterized the Shakers, whose plans have always in view the passing of each individual into his or her right position, and of providing a suitable, pleasant, and profitable employment for every one."[115] In order to bring this division of labor to its perfection, making themselves the ideal tools of the community, nameless interchangeable parts of the social machine, they had abolished all private property. Although "many errors still cling here," they avoided "that fatal one of property involvements with the old world."[116] For all their valuing of skill and craftsmanship, no Shaker ever claimed any product as his own, not even to the extent of signing a creation so that others might admire his skill. The life was tribal, and, as Lane noticed with pleasure, the community seemed to function instinctively. He told Emerson that their "daily arrangements" were "nervous. Without any formal communication they coincide, and·when one is ready, others are, and the cart & the horse also."[117] Even in the consociate family at Fruitlands, Lane had specified the need for members "who know instinctively what is to be done, who want little outward direction and instruction, and who need no looking after."[118] With the Shakers he found the perfection of this "nervous" organization of society. As the division of labor became instinctive, so the need to distinguish mine and thine would also vanish. There was to be a concurrent advance from the joint-stock company to the complete community of goods. Self would fade into the group will.

5. Family versus Community

All this is the very antithesis of the transcendentalist solution. "Alas for the hermits when that day comes!" cried Emerson. "Alas for the Family! When all are rich we shall cry for poverty dear poverty again."[119] The most difficult bit of analysis for Lane was surely that which dealt with and disposed of the family. All these ideas had been brewing in his head during the final months of Fruitlands, when it began to appear to him that the "universal" and the "natural" family were incompatible. At the end of December 1843, a "Social Reform Convention" was held in Boston, which both Alcott and Lane attended. Alcott, though invited to speak, "had no disposition, he said, to do so."[120] The collapse of the community had depressed his spirits. Lane, on the other hand, was full of conclusions from their experiment, and he not only addressed the convention, but also began a series of articles on his discoveries.[121] In these the development of his position on the family in community can be traced.

No doubt Lane's inclination was, from the first, toward sexual chastity. "We are learning," he said at one point, "to keep our hands from each other's bodies."[122] Perhaps Shaker celibacy attracted him more than Shaker communism. But as a disciple of Pestalozzi, Lane had an obligation to put the family, and especially the mother, in a central place in his scheme of universal love, and as late as his 1843 article on "Social Tendencies," one can see him struggling with his changing views: "The family then need not be a hindrance to a love for the whole human race," he faltered.[123] By the next issue of *The Dial* he wondered cautiously, "Is it questioned whether the family arrangement of mankind is to be preserved?"[124] By March 1844 he was sure: "Now, marriage, as at present constituted, is most decidedly an individual, and not a universal act. It is an individual act, too, of a depreciated and selfish kind. The spouse is an expansion and enlargement of one's self, and the children participate of the same nature. The all-absorbent influence of this union is too obvious to be dwelt upon. It is used to justify every glaring and cruel act of selfish acquisition. It is made the ground-work of the institution of property, which is itself the foundation of so many evils. This institution of property and its numerous auxiliaries must be abrogated in associative life; or it will be little better than isolate life."[125]

Opinions like these, of course, were what led Lane's later critics to accuse him of attempting to poison the Alcott matrimonial well. But Lane had not arrived at Fruitlands with these views fully formed and ready to be wielded. They had developed there, and not only in his mind, but also in Bronson Alcott's — and, for that matter, in Abigail Alcott's. The issue was not the truth or falsity of the theory, but the course of action to be followed after recognizing its consequences. Alcott seems finally to have agreed with Lane's formulation, that "in those maternal affections, and their consequences in living offspring, there is an element so subversive of general association that the two cannot co-exist."[126] But when it came to the alternatives, Fruitlands or Abigail, his choice was for the isolated rather than the consociate family. Once separated from Lane, he threw himself into its bosom, much to Mrs. Alcott's admiration. At first there were some efforts to scout out an alternative experiment, at Brook Farm, Hopedale, or Northampton, but both Alcotts decided they "must take up the family cross and work on, isolated and poor, a while longer."[127] These are Mrs. Alcott's words, and one detects a certain grim relief in them. The Shakers had not impressed her — "There is servitude somewhere, I have no doubt" — and other communities threatened "an unwarrantable alienation from our children."[128] For Mrs. Alcott at least, the "family cross" was chosen more than it was borne.

Whatever Alcott's own feelings, he began to make his ideology fit his new practice. There was a period of deep depression, and then some thought of a second Fruitlands on the land that Emerson and Mrs. Alcott's relatives had provided. Lane was invited, with what result we have already seen. But of all those persons he considered as prospective collaborators, Alcott seems to have been most eager to secure his youngest brother Junius and their aged mother, who lived with him. "It is quite unlikely that others will unite with us, especially at first," he wrote Junius. "Few, perhaps not a solitary soul, is ready for such an enterprize; How far we are ourselves remains to be proved to us by actual trial. If a Holy Family is beyond us, we may, at least, exclude much that annoys and renders uncomely the Households on which we cast our eyes wheresoever we turn — on the world around us."[129] The intensity of desire here, to affirm the "natural" family in any new undertaking, is underlined by the fact that he importuned his brother seven times that year — as many (surviving) letters as he had written to Junius in all the preceding years. After this effort to reconstitute his own childhood family,[130] Alcott never again contemplated communal life. As he wrote Lane a few years later, "The Comforter enters only through the doors of the Private Heart into the Private House to gladden the Family Circle."[131] Bold words to his former associate in establishing a universal, not a private family. Many years later he wrote even more dogmatically, "I have long since questioned the fitness of any considerable number of persons for Community life. A School is a possibility. Yet any separation from parents, for any long time, seems undesirable unless in case of their unfitness to have charge of their children. The family is *the unit* around which all social endeavors should organize, if we would succeed in educating men for the true ends of existence. And the cooperation of women in the practical working out is indispensable."[132] Thus did Alcott argue himself out of the range of Charles Lane's fervent example. However attracted by monastic ideals, however unsparing he himself had proved during the ascetic days at Fruitlands, Alcott found that the universal community asked more than he could give.

Emerson, who published everything that Lane wrote for *The Dial* on these touchy subjects, was intrigued by Lane's analysis. He understood perfectly well what Lane and others would have of him. He would have it of himself, but "I allow the old circumstance of mother, wife, children, and brother to overpower my wish to right myself with absolute Nature; and I also consent to hang, a parasite, with all the parasites on this rotten system of property." Although he did not think that a colony the size of Brook Farm was necessary or conducive to those reforms, several years before Fruitlands he had had "the dream that a small family of ascetics, working together on a secluded spot, would keep each other's benevolence and invention awake, so that we should every day fall on good hints and more beautiful methods."[133] His summerhouse of 1847 was a faded afterimage of that dream.

From the highest ground, then, he agreed with Lane and the Shakers, though he saw their encampment no nearer to the summit than Thoreau's: "it is honest & intelligent to say, (Shaker or hermit) I am clear that in the state of prayer I neither marry, nor vote, nor buy, nor sell: I have experiences that are above all civil or nuptial or commercial relations: and I wish to vow myself to those. If you ask how the world is to get on, &c. &c. I have no answer. I do not care for such cattle of consequences. It is not my question, it is your own; answer it who will: I am contented with this new & splendid revelation of the One, and will not dispute."[134] Yet in almost the same breath

he must account for his failure — even greater than Alcott's —
to live up to any such vision: "I am nominally a believer: yet I
hold on to property: I eat my bread with unbelief. I approve
every wild action of the experimenters. I say what they say
concerning celibacy or money or community of goods and my
only apology for not doing their work is preoccupation of
mind. I have a work of my own which I know I can do with
some success. It would leave that undone if I should undertake
with them and I do not see in myself any vigour equal to such
an enterprise. . . . This is belief too, this debility of practices,
this staying by our work. For the obedience to a man's genius is
the *particular* of Faith: by & by, shall come the *Universal* of
Faith."[135]

Emerson had visited the Shakers several times, and they
appear frequently enough in his journals to suggest more than
idle curiosity. After one visit, which he made in the company of
Isaac Hecker — still looking for a community to match his own
intensity — Emerson concluded: "I judge the whole society to
be a cleanly & industrious but stupid people."[136] There is a
relation between this criticism and Emerson's difficulty in
living up to his own "splendid revelation of the One." In the end
he always gave his work, his vocation for writing, as the excuse
for ignoring all other calls. It was his "genius," the contribution
that he could make, whatever he ought to do. When he condemned the Shakers' stupidity or called them "peasants, with a
squalid contentment,"[137] he was once again valuing the life of
the mind over the social and economic welfare of the community. Shakers were prolific inventors and fine craftsmen, but
their arts and sciences were entirely communal, part of their
social life and the economy of the village. Emerson was a
philosopher and poet, and the economies of his calling were
quite different. It was his view "that if a man find in himself any
strong bias to poetry, to art, to the contemplative life, drawing
him to these things with a devotion incompatible with good
husbandry, that man ought to reckon early with himself, and,
respecting the compensations of the Universe, ought to ransom

himself from the duties of economy, by a certain rigor and privation in his habits."[138] This ascetism was Thoreauvian rather than Shaker and involved a shift from his earlier advocacy of manual labor, which, whatever its virtues, he had now decided was destructive of the writing impulse.

Emerson had identified the risk in thinking about the advantages and disadvantages of manual labor — both the experience of the Brook Farmers ("We have no thoughts") and his own discoveries in the garden (it "indisposes & disqualifies for intellectual exertion").[139] That lesson had hidden ramifications for the debate between community and individualism. If it was necessary to the work of the mind that the work of the body be reduced, one alternative might be to join a community in which good planning and the division of labor conserved energy for higher purposes. But the examples of Brook Farm and the Shakers suggested that even if such a savings might ultimately be achieved, the communal life itself was dangerous to private thought. At the other extreme was the "hut," which provided a sure defense against the group-mind and tribal unanimity, so that one was not simply an instinctual member, but an entire, conscious individual — Man.

Yet here he came up against the characteristic impasse of his situation, for his own "genius" seemed to call him to be less than Man — merely "Man Thinking." Alcott once told him he thought the race would eventually shed its trunk and become merely a head, a brain, a consciousness, and Thoreau had said, "My head is hands and feet. I feel all my best faculties concentrated in it."[140] Already Emerson had questioned his "right to my fingers or toes. If a palsy should mortify them it were just."[141] He himself was part of the division of labor, and willing as he might be to give up the advantages he received from those who represented arms and legs, he could not relinquish his own role in the scheme.

Ultimately he found a solution, in theory if not in practice. It might not be necessary, he decided, to go through all the actual maneuvers of the farmer in order to attain his integrity.

"I suppose that all that is done in ploughing & sowing & reaping & storing is repeated in finer sort in the life of men who never touch the plough handles. The essence of those manipulations is subtle & reappears in countinghouses & council boards, in games of cards & chess, in conversations, correspondences, & in poets' rhymes. . . . The good of doing with one's own hands is the honouring of the symbol. My own cooking, my own cobbling, fencebuilding, digging of a well, building of a house, twisting of a rope, forging of a hoe & shovel, — is poetic."[142] So, while in 1841 he had said, "Better that the book should not be quite so good, and the bookmaker abler and better,"[143] by 1845 he had begun to think that he might have both, symbolically. Symbols, after all, were his vocation.

At bottom then, it was not simply family ties that kept any transcendentalist out of the communities. Lane had touched the nerve when he described the family as a kind of property, "an expansion and enlargement of one's self." In Lane's final analysis, he viewed the family, "isolate life," and the institution of property as a single syndrome, deeply opposed to the community of goods, persons, and spirit of the "true life." This is especially important because it helps show the connection between a "family man" like Alcott or Emerson and a "hermit" like Thoreau, identifying all three as enemies of the Shaker model of the good society.

6. Tribe versus Hermit

Although much attracted by Thoreau's asceticism, Lane early recognized him as an archetype of the individualist he was struggling against. A year before Thoreau went down to the pond, Lane was already preparing an answer to his example. In his "Life in the Woods" (later the subtitle of the first edition of

Walden) Lane wrote, "Even now we hear of some individuals, on whom the world might hopefully rely to become eminent even amongst the worthy, betaking themselves from the busy haunts of men to a more select and secluded life."[144] After reviewing the advantages of a "sylvan life," Lane concludes in terms that, ten years later, would have served for a detailed criticism of *Walden*:

> Poetic wanderings will not more rectify us than trading conversations. And on calm consideration, unswayed by those paradoxes which ingenious men have from time to time constructed concerning the beautiful liberty of sylvan life, and to which imaginations we have on this occasion perhaps too strongly tended, have we not to confess that one is as distant from true life as the other? They both lie on the same circumference. They are but segments of one circle, struck by the compasses of human selfishness at too great a distance from the true centre.[145]

Even the limited motive of the scholar, the desire for "uninterrupted seclusion," was unlikely to be satisfied: "By the time the hut is built, the rudest furniture constructed, the wood chopped, the fire burning, the bread grown and prepared, the whole time will be exhausted, and no interval remain for comfortably clothing the body, for expansion in art, or for recreation by the book or pen." Thoreau proved him wrong in his arithmetic, but perhaps he was right when he remarked "that solitude is a state suitable only to the best or the worst."[146]

Thoreau's hut represented more than "poetic wanderings," however. It stood for the whole range of answers to the Shaker example — not merely intense individual consciousness versus the "nervous" instinctual teamwork of a "tribal" society, but also the principle of property and land instead of the factory, joint-stock communism, and the division of labor; the complete and self-reliant man against the mere tool of the system; and finally, the single isolated family as opposed to the universal one. No doubt Thoreau seems an odd representative of institutions like private property or the family. Emerson would be a more likely specimen, as owner not only of his own house and land but also of the plot on which Thoreau's hut stood, not to mention his share in Alcott's "Hillside." Furthermore, both Alcott and Emerson had "the old circumstance of mother, wife, children, and brother" to hinder and clog their communal aspirations, insofar as they had them. As it happens, however, Thoreau was loyal to his own versions of hearth and home. Although he may have had few literal dependents, he was not without "circumstance." He was the most easily made homesick of the three, and least likely to stray for long from his familiar haunts. One forgets too easily, in considering Thoreau's lengthy residence with the Emersons, or his two years by the pond, that most of his life he remained in the bosom of his family — father, mother, sisters, brother, aunts. His passion for sauntering and sojourning had its counterbalance in his inveterate domesticity. As for property, it was not important whether he or Emerson held the deed to Walden, or passed it on to heirs; Thoreau was the sole proprietor of his domain, and found a dozen metaphors that put him in possession of goods without the nuisance of paying taxes on them. This view of property may be appreciated by comparing it with the opposite attitude that prevailed at Brook Farm. There they had supposed that their paper ownership of shares of stock made them upholders of the institution of private property, whereas in fact they lumped all for the public good. Thoreau owned his land more than any Brook Farmer his. When he was ready to leave, he got his investment out as easily as he had put it in — something Hawthorne wished he could do.

Thoreau's whole conception of ownership was as "an expansion and enlargement of one's self," carrying Lane's formulation to its extreme. Imagination "enjoyed the most valuable part of a farm."[147] Indeed, his imagination gobbled up every scrap of life as if there would be no second helpings. He and Emerson once had an argument about property which ended with Emerson saying, "We have literary property. The very recording of a thought betrays a distrust that there is any more or much more as good for us."[148] One wonders how much of this Emerson actually said to Thoreau. In any case, he concluded his journal entry in a Thoreauvian vein himself: "Why should a man spend years upon the carving an Apollo who looked Apollos into the landscape with every glance he threw?"[149] A good question for the young man who, almost as early as this (1838), had begun to think of himself as Apollo in servitude, tending the property of King Admetus. A dozen years later Thoreau was still trying to redeem the mortgaged universe: "What if a man were earnestly and wisely to set about recollecting and preserving the thoughts which he has had! How many perchance are now irrecoverable!" he exclaims. In comic desperation he imagines "Calling in his neighbors to aid him."[150] If any man ever had neighbors adept at such collecting, he did; but that was just the point, that no one could help him amass the fortune that he had in mind. Family and friends, field or hut, all were mere raw materials of consciousness.

It was just this concern with self that seemed most retrograde to Charles Lane. Thoreau's intention in going off to Walden was to gather his life into a bundle, figuratively and literally. He designed to live off his own efforts exclusively. This meant building his own shack, hoeing his own beans, choosing his own time. It meant pulling things together in the imagination, keeping a journal where he might cultivate his "literary property" as well. His principle was, "Do what nobody else can do for you. Omit to do anything else."[151] To Charles Lane, all this was an utterly selfish perversion of both nature and economics, an anarchist division of labor that would leave man alone in a solipsistic universe. The true "child of nature," Lane argued, is not solitary, but "moves in a circle much more social than modern cities can boast. The tribe is a better type of the universal family than the city, where the inhabitants of the same street are frequently unknown to each other after dwelling many years side by side." The hermit was a product of this intermediate civilization and would vanish as society progressed. "By union of numbers, by condensation into a phalanx, the white man conquers the red, whom singly he could never subdue. By a new and superior phalanx, constructed altogether on a different basis, it is probably destined that the present civilized institutions shall be superseded, and the new and superior nature in man receive a new and superior development."[152] And so Lane came back again to the Shakers and their community of universal love, at the extreme pole from Thoreau's individual self-communion.

While Lane was elaborating these distinctions between the solitary hermit and the primitive tribe, another student of human nature had been conducting original researches into related questions. His results may serve as a concluding example of a communal way of life and the transcendental response to it. Herman Melville's sojourn with the cannibals had taken place during the summer of 1842, and by 1846 his adventures were in print as *Typee, A Peep at Polynesian Life*. American communitists found Melville's South Sea paradise full of utopian notions, further evidence to support what they already believed, that there was a necessary connection between material abundance and social virtues. *Typee* was immediately reviewed by Charles Dana in the Brook Farm newspaper, where, in making his Fourierist point, he quoted these interesting passages, among others:

> . . . there were no legal provisions whatever for the well-being and conservation of society, the enlightened end of civilized legislation. And yet every thing went on in the valley with a harmony and smoothness unparalleled, I will venture to assert, in the most select, refined, and pious associations of mortals in Christendom. . . .
>
> There was one admirable trait in the general character of the Typees which, more than anything else, secured my admiration: it was the unanimity of feeling they displayed on every occasion. With them there hardly appeared to be any difference of opinion upon any subject whatever. They all thought and acted alike. I do not conceive that they could

> support a debating society for a single night: there would be nothing to dispute about; and were they to call a convention to take into consideration the state of the tribe, its session would be a remarkably short one. They showed this spirit of unanimity in every action of life; every thing was done in concert and good fellowship.
>
> During my whole stay on the island I never witnessed a single quarrel, nor anything that in the slightest degree approached even to a dispute. The natives appeared to form one household, whose members were bound together by the ties of strong affection. The love of kindred I did not so much perceive, for it seemed blended in the general love; and where all were treated as brothers and sisters, it was hard to tell who were actually related to each other by blood.[153]

It is not easy to determine Melville's opinion of all this, but Dana's delighted and unconditional approval is evident. He sees nothing problematic in the Typee unanimity, but is only concerned to recreate it in America, by means of "A social system which will produce and distribute to every member of society a complete abundance as the result of a healthy amount of labor."[154] It never occurs to him that the Typees might have flourished so far, not so much because of the abundance of food, as because they were insulated, geographically and intellectually, from civilization's property and diseases, vices and laws. Perhaps they retained their peace and prosperity because they "thought as one," no individual ever entertaining an idea that could possibly be subversive to the tribal order — thus matching the internalized discipline of the Shakers. Again one encounters the limited perspective of the Brook Farmers. Lane would have seen the connections between the instinctual infallibility, the unanimity, the peacefulness, and the predominance of tribal over kinship ties, the universal over the isolated family. These were the traits of the Shakers too, enhanced by Christianity and celibacy.

Emerson would have worried about the other side of the story — not merely the "nervous" unanimity of mind, but also the "squalid contentment." The price of salvation from the alienated and tainted world of the nineteenth century was not to be paid in the most cherished currency of transcendentalism, the individual consciousness itself.

Alcott on the other hand seemed tempted by the eternal valley where all are equally kin and no exclusive loves could make men into brooding, possessive self-devourers. When he read *Typee* in 1846, he "almost found myself embarked to spend the rest of my days with those simple islanders of the South Seas."[155] The sentiment was one his friends would scarcely have been able to comprehend, and his course, like theirs, had always lain on an opposite bearing. If an island was to be the metaphor instead of a hut, then the original of Robinson Crusoe's island, Juan Fernandez, was more like it, where one might keep both a journal and a closer watch on oneself. Indeed, once in his journal Alcott used the name as a kind of synonym for his utopia: "Evening, Samuel Bower, one of my Fruitlanders is here, and discusses ideas as believingly as ever for Juan-Fernandez."[156] Alcott was often confused about his own aims and ideals, as his Fruitlands waverings show, but he finally had an ear more for Thoreau's flute than Lane's. Carlyle, who differed from the transcendentalists in valuing community over the individual, was nasty but accurate in his characterization of Alcott: "His aim is, it would seem, to *be* something, and become a universal blessing thereby; my fixed long-growing conviction is that a man had better not attempt to *be* anything, but struggle with the whole soul of him to *do* something. . . . I do not want another Simon Stylites, however cunning his *pillar* may be."[157] There were two religious alternatives — the monastic fellowship of the primitive church, or the holy hermitage of the desert. One was an act of becoming, establishing the Kingdom in the here and now, a City on a Hill. The other was an ecstatic vision, a feat of identity.

When it came to feats of identity, Thoreau was the most agile of the transcendentalists, and Lane, attracted to him as he was, knew him for the enemy. Thoreau in his turn was wary of communal joys. Even the Indians that he so much admired, he admired only singly, Indian file. One does not find him praising tribal life, as Lane does, and in *The Maine Woods* his version of tropical paradise is the cold and misty top of Mt. Ktaadn, which he climbed alone, jilted by his drunken Indian guides, and outstripping his white companions. "Only daring and insolent men, perchance, go there," he mused on the ascent. "Simple races, as savages, do not climb mountains."[158]

On the way back down, "we were startled by seeing, on a little sandy shelf by the side of the stream, the fresh print of a man's foot, and for a moment realized how Robinson Crusoe felt in a similar case."[159] As it turned out, the track had been made by one of the party on the approach. But Thoreau — whose account of his own self-marooning at Walden has always appealed to the same type of imagination as *Robinson Crusoe* — was on the lookout for such footprints. There is another one in the journals, "the track of a bare human foot in the dusty road, the toes and muscles all faithfully imprinted. Such a sight is so rare that it affects me with surprise, as the footprint on the shore of Juan Fernandez did Crusoe. It is equally rare here. I am affected as if some Indian or South-Sea-Islander had been along, some man who had a foot."[160] Thoreau managed to turn that occasion into a routine condemnation of social roles — "It is possible for a man wholly to disappear and be merged in his manners"[161] — but more significant even than his antipathy for such civilized role-playing is his evident enjoyment in simply discovering the footprint. Thoreau's writings are full of little discoveries like this — messages left in his hut, tracks of moose, abandoned campsites, signs of spring. He is Crusoe on the island, Adam in the garden, poking around amidst the unexplored and unnamed universe, uncovering tokens that suggest it was made just for him.

Food for Thought

Suppose you have reformed & live on grains &
black birch bark & muddy water that you may
have leisure; well, what then? What will you
do with the long day? think? — what! all day?

Emerson's *Journals*

1. Speculators

In periods of widespread agitation for reform, like the 1830s and 1840s, there is a point at which disillusionment and skepticism begin to set in, whatever the "successes" of the movement. Charles Lane, an ex-businessman as well as a utopian enthusiast, enjoyed an especially high-angle view of American reform movements. He drew attention to the backlash of alienation in an essay he published in *The Dial* for 1843, entitled "Social Tendencies": "Political reform succeeds political reform, and men are no better — and no happier. Education proceeds, and with it, penitentiaries and jails, hospitals and insane asylums are multiplied. . . . The consciousness of such results frequently drives men back to individual narrowness. In his fruitless reliance, the publicist turns misanthrope. In contemplation of perverse humanity, the mentalist sinks into the book-collector, the literary critic, or the speculatist."[1]

It was a tendency, especially as regards "mentalists" and "speculatists," that Emerson also noticed, in his "Lectures on

117

the Times" of 1841-42; he described the result as he saw it among his friends:

> The genius of the day does not incline to a deed, but to a beholding. It is not that men do not wish to act; they pine to be employed, but are paralyzed by the uncertainty what they should do. The inadequacy of the work to the faculties, is the painful perception which keeps them still. This happens to the best. Then, talents bring their usual temptations, and the current literature and poetry with perverse ingenuity draws us away from life to solitude and meditation. This could be well borne, if it were great and involuntary; if the men were ravished by their thought, and hurried into ascetic extravagances. Society could then manage to release their shoulder from its wheel, and grant them for a time this privilege of sabbath. But they are not so. Thinking, which was a rage, is become an art.[2]

In the journal entry that gave rise to this paragraph Emerson had included himself among these solitary thinkers: "Yet is it not ridiculous this that we do in this languid idle trick that we have gradually fallen into of writing & writing without an end. After a day of humiliation & stripes if I can write it down I am straightway relieved & can sleep well. After a day of joy the beating heart is calmed again by the diary. If grace is given me by all angels & I pray, if then I can catch one ejaculation of humility or hope & set it down in syllables, devotion is at an end."[3] When he worked the passage into his lecture, Emerson first removed everything personal and then softened the criticism itself, advising his readers to "have a little patience with this melancholy humor. . . . By the side of these men, the hot agitators have a certain cheap and ridiculous air; they even look smaller than the others. Of the two, I own, I like the speculators best" — as well he might, since they were his closest friends: Henry Thoreau, Bronson Alcott, and other transcendentalists, not to mention Emerson himself. He ended with an announcement of a "new order" of society to be created by

these unnamed but increasingly well-known "speculators":
"The revolutions that impend over society are not now from
ambition and rapacity, from impatience of one or another
form of government, but from new modes of thinking, which
shall recompose society after a new order, which shall animate
labor by love and science, which shall destroy the value of
many kinds of property, and replace all property within the
dominion of reason and equity."

The "modes of thinking" Emerson had in mind were not a
matter of "new ideas," nor the invention of practical solutions
to the problems of the age. That was the province of the
reformers. These "modes" were more on the order of what is
sometimes called today "new consciousness" — a term Emerson himself used when looking back on the period in "Historic
Notes of Life and Letters in New England."[4] The transcendentalist's object in retreating into "solitude and meditation" was
to reexamine the laws of human existence — physical, moral,
and spiritual. Society was at such a crisis as to require a whole
new theory of medicine before a cure might be prescribed.

Of the three Concord neighbors, only Emerson always
maintained this rather lofty perspective. Thoreau and Alcott
were equally dedicated researchers into transcendental truth,
but less concerned to analyze their projects. They thought of
themselves as subjects of experiment, not as historical objects,
and they played Aylmer or Ethan Brand to Emerson's Hawthorne. Alcott's commune at Fruitlands and Thoreau's shack
on Walden Pond were the laboratories. Emerson's study was
the workshop where the results could be carefully collated and
stored in time capsules.

"The young men were born with knives in their brain,"
Emerson wrote in "Historic Notes," with "a tendency to intro-
version, self-dissection, anatomizing of motives."[5] Even he fell
into the scientific metaphor. One must not think of the journals
of the transcendentalists as merely the record of their experiments, however — the journals *were* the experiment, and what
one might be tempted to call the "subject" of those journals, the

reportable life, was mere circumstance, a set of occasions for thought. If Thoreau was in himself "a practical refutation of socialism,"[6] as Emerson delighted in saying, this did not mean that living in a hut was a political answer to Fruitlands or Brook Farm. *Walden* was Thoreau's answer, not Walden. And *Walden* was, essentially, his journal.

It is not quite right to think of these journals as writings in the usual sense, addressed to an audience and published. Although *Walden* was published, and although Alcott would have been happy to match the innumerable essays and lectures Emerson mined from his own journals, that was not the point. These journals might make interesting reading in many forms, but their essence was not a message. It was, as Emerson said, a "new mode of thinking." To understand this more fully, it may be helpful to consider the journalizing of the three in the metaphoric light of an activity to which they gave a good deal more thought than scientific experiment. Bizarre as it may at first seem, there is much to be learned from a comparison of their habits of writing with their habits of eating; and that comparison is the purpose of this chapter.

2. Dietary Laws

The subject was popular. Diet was a reform movement as much as was nonresistance or abolitionism, and had its sects and schisms — Grahamism, water-cure (which *banned* water, among other things), Pythagoreanism, and so on. Alcott's cousin William proved that he could do without water for an entire year, and a lady at Modern Times was said to have died of a diet of beans. On this crowded bandwagon "health," "temperance," and "economy" were the chief banners, but obviously any such search for new dietary laws also had an underlying religious meaning. For some comprehensive thinkers, diet was the central wheel in the intricate watchworks of the social order; every tooth had to be counted and geared into the rest of life. If, for example, one ate meat, it was necessary to swallow all the prior arrangements and by-products of that taste — pastures and fences, forage crops and stable duties, manure to fertilize and oxen to plough, milk and tallow and leather, butchers and ovens, whole vocabularies of flesh and blood. To some like Bronson Alcott and Charles Lane, co-founders of Fruitlands, it was clear that men would be better off without any of these advantages. Life was simpler and cleaner in the vegetable world. At Brook Farm, Lane noted with disgust, "They buy butter to the extent of 500 dollars a year."[7] At Fruitlands they required nothing, in field or stable, pantry or memory, but what would garnish their bread and apples.

Even at Brook Farm they could calculate the place of diet in an economy, and in the "retrenchment" years of Fourierism they went without meat, tea, butter, and sugar, in order to cut down expenses.[8] Emerson, always more sympathetic to the Brook Farm than the Fruitlands temperament, would have understood both the indulgence and the retrenchment in West Roxbury. One of the upshots of his long-pondered decision that manual labor was uncongenial to the contemplative man was this advice to poets: "Let him learn to eat his meals standing, and to like the taste of fair water & black bread."[9] Or again, more personally: "It is time to have the thing looked into & with a transpiercing criticism settled whether life is worth having on such terms. If not, let us eat less food & less, & clear ourselves of such a fool's universe. I will not stay, for one, longer than I am contented."[10] This was somewhere in between Thoreauvian simplicity and Brook Farm expedience, certainly far from the asceticism of Fruitlands.

In his youth Emerson had fasted with a certain zeal, though not quite the passion of his neighbors in later life. His motive was partly ascetic, very like theirs. When he asked, "was ever the full feeder ready for religion?" he was foreshadowing Alcott's moralistic eating; when he told himself, "It were well to live purely, to make your word worth something. Deny yourself cake & ale to make your testimony irresistible," he sounded just like his young disciple Thoreau twenty years later.[11] But his impulse was experimental as much as it was self-denying, and once the lesson was learned, the rigors might cease. "Every sane man has tried starving," he wrote years afterward, "& found that it did not give him blood but that we were faint & dispirited."[12] He toyed with vegetarianism more than once — "I begin to dislike animal food"[13] he noted in 1840 — but ultimately he preferred Thoreau's Epicurean maxims to the Pythagorean manifestos of Lane and Alcott. "The man that shoots a buffalo, lives better than he who boards at the Graham House said H. T.," or "I like Henry Thoreau's statement on Diet. 'If a man does not believe that he can thrive on board nails, I will not talk with him.'"[14]

This latter saying finally got into *Walden*, where Thoreau devoted much of his first chapter on "Economy" to the relations between diet and manual labor. As with the other bodily necessities he recognized, shelter and clothing and fuel, he was chiefly interested in finding the most direct and uncomplicated ratio between effort and result, desire and fulfillment. He chose to need less, in kind and quantity, in order to expend less energy acquiring it. "I learned from my two years' experience that it would cost incredibly little trouble to obtain one's necessary food, even in this latitude; that a man may use as simple a diet as the animals, and yet retain health and strength."[15] The corollary, "Like work, like diet," was expressed in his journal for 1853, when he was doing "coarse and hurried outdoor work": "Left to my chosen pursuit, I should never drink tea nor coffee, nor eat meat. The diet of any class is the natural result of its employment and locality."[16] On the trail, as may be seen from advice he gave T. W. Higginson and others who inquired about provisioning their excursions in the woods, Thoreau ate almost a half-pound of meat to his pound of bread per day — not counting fish and game, nor side dishes like rice and sugar.[17] But at Walden he ate only a bit of pork and fish from the pond; cereals were his staples. For twenty-seven cents a week, he had all he wanted of "rye and Indian meal without yeast, potatoes, rice, a very little salt pork, molasses, and salt."[18] A few delicacies, like chestnuts and berries, do not appear in the ledger.

An interesting gloss on these computations occurs in "Higher Laws," where Thoreau adds in the noneconomic values:

> . . . there is something essentially unclean about this diet and all flesh, and I began to see where housework commences, and whence the endeavor, which costs so much, to wear a tidy and respectable appearance each day, to keep the house sweet and free from all ill odors and sights. Having been my own butcher and scullion and cook, as well as the gentleman for whom the dishes were served up, I can speak from an unusually complete experience. The practical objection to animal food in my case was its uncleanness; and, besides, when I had caught and cleaned and cooked and eaten my fish, they seemed not to have fed me essentially. It was insignificant and unnecessary, and cost more than it came to. A little bread or a few potatoes would have done as well, with less trouble and filth. Like many of my contemporaries, I had rarely for many years used animal food, or tea, or coffee, &c.; not so much because of any ill effects which I had traced to them, as because they were not agreeable to my imagination. The repugnance to animal food is not the effect of experience, but is an instinct.[19]

Here we have the beginnings of the "higher laws" that connect diet and keeping a journal, both occasions for invoking the spiritual life. The "essential food" that would be "agreeable to my imagination" — what is that? "Who has not sometimes derived an inexpressible satisfaction from his food in which appetite had no share? I have been thrilled to think that I owed a mental perception to the commonly gross sense of taste, that I have been inspired through the palate, that some berries which I had eaten on a hill-side had fed my genius."[20] This merely hints at the spiritual sustenance Thoreau had in mind, but it will serve to suggest something further until more of the context of his experiments in diet has been discussed.

Alcott was one of the contemporaries Thoreau referred to, who for over fifty years abstained from meat. His motives, like Thoreau's, began with the imagination and extended to the scullery. One of the mottoes he used to put on his family's plates at mealtimes read, "Apollo eats no flesh and has no beard, his voice is melody itself."[21] But Alcott's chief vegetarian aims were moral rather than poetic, as is clear in the broadside of the summer of 1843 announcing the establishment of Fruitlands:

> It is calculated that if no animal food were consumed, one-fourth of the land now used would suffice for human sustenance. And the extensive tracts of country now appropriated to grazing, mowing, and other modes of animal provision, could be cultivated by and for intelligent and affectionate human neighbors. The sty and the stable too often secure more of the farmer's regard than he bestows on the garden and the children. No hope is there for humanity while Woman is withdrawn from the tender assiduities which adorn her and her household to the servitudes of the dairy and the flesh pots. . . .
> Debauchery of both the earthly soil and the human body is the result of this cattle keeping. The land is scourged for crops to feed the animals, whose ordures are used under the erroneous supposition of restoring lost fertility; disease is thus infused into the human body; stimulants and medicines are resorted to for relief, which end in a precipitation of the original evil to a more disastrous depth. These misfortunes which affect not only the body, but by reaction rise to the sphere of the soul, would be avoided, or at least in part, by the disuse of animal food. Our diet is therefore strictly the pure and bloodless kind.[22]

Admirers of Alcott, while accepting his own diet as a benign eccentricity, have tended to regard Fruitlands as a wild masochistic extravagance, largely to be attributed to the baleful influence of Charles Lane, not only in the ticklish area of domestic relations, but also in the extension of the vegetarian regimen to all the members of the Alcott family. The chief evidence cited is Mrs. Alcott's journal entry of 22 August 1842, essentially a sigh of relief at her husband's (later to be reversed) decision that his friends Wright and Lane would not return with him from England: "It seemed premature," she wrote, "more particularly as we are not favorably situated here for any experiments of diet — having little or no fruit on the place, no house-room, and surrounded by those whose prejudices are intolerable."[23] While Mrs. Alcott's reluctance is obviously enough an anticipation of hardship (in addition to everything else, she had very bad teeth, and hated cooking), she does not seem to blame the as yet unseen English ascetics. If they come, there is to be an experiment, entirely of her husband's undertaking so far as any evidence in her journal can go to show.

Alcott was so full of his vegetables at this time, that he needed no Charles Lane to incite him. Carlyle impatiently reported one of their interviews to Emerson: "I do esteem his Potatoe-gospel a mere imbecillity which *cannot* be discussed in this busy world at this time of day. . . ." Emerson apologized: "It is a new thing with him, this eating better than his neighbors, & I could heartily wish he had either not come to it, or had gotten through it, before he saw you. . . ."[24] As Emerson well knew, Alcott's vegetarianism was not of recent date — he had quit eating meat in his mid-thirties — though he had only recently begun to make quite such a fuss about it. Of course that was the point, to make a virtue of it, eating *better* than his neighbors. Everything about Alcott's vegetarianism was flavored with moral enterprise, a decisive renunciation for the sake of diminishing evil and promoting good in the world —

with the emphasis on diminishing. "Man's victory over nature and himself is to overcome the brute beast in him."[25] Thus he spoke at various times of the "virtues of plants" and the "vice of intemperance," which could be remedied by "a more chaste and salutory diet."[26]

One day in 1839, before he had met Charles Lane or thought of requiring that his family imitate his vegetarianism, he was asked, presumably by Mrs. Alcott, to stop by the butcher and pick out a "flitch" of meat for dinner. The butcher apparently took advantage of Alcott's uneasiness in the shop, and sold him the wrong (more expensive?) portion — for which Alcott was blamed at home. His journal entry is agitated:

> What have I to do with butchers? Am I to go smelling about markets? Both are an offence to me. Death yawns at me as I walk up and down in this abode of skulls. Murder and blood are written on its stalls. Cruelty stares at me from the butcher's face. I tread amidst carcasses. I am in the presence of the slain. The death-set eyes of beasts peer at me and accuse me of belonging to the race of murderers. Quartered, disembowelled creatures on suspended hooks plead with me. I feel myself dispossessed of the divinity. I am a replenisher of grave yards. I prowl, amidst other unclean spirits and voracious demons, for my prey.[27]

In all his writings, nowhere does Alcott's disgust with meat come through more authentically, yet even here the voice of morality drowns out that of instinct. The terms of his revulsion are ethical and even legal — "offence," "murder," "cruelty," "accuse me," "plead with me," "dispossessed of the divinity." No matter how close he got to it, blood was still an ethical concept to him. Even Thoreau's "practical objection to animal food" — its "uncleanness" — has here been transferred from the meat itself to those "unclean spirits" who, Alcott among them, "prowl" among the "slain." The scene is dramatic — stagey — but that seems a rhetorical effect and not a matter of either imagination or deep feeling.

The truth of the matter is that Alcott's vegetarianism, as much else in his life, was programmatic. His utopian ideal was no spa of health and comradeship. The abstemious Charles Lane himself, who sneered at the "joyous frivolous manner" of the Brook Farmers, was awed by the stringencies developing at Fruitlands. He wrote his friends back in England that Alcott's "high requirements" had scared off more potential consociates than the diet itself, "a test quite sufficient for many." Alcott made everything an occasion for trial and victory. "To do better and better, to *be* better and better is the constant theme. His hand is everywhere, like his mind."[28] He took over the cooking and supervised the eating. It became an event worthy of remark in twelve-year-old Anna Alcott's diary when her mother made the bread.[29] By precept and example her father impressed upon the children that every activity ought to be turned to some good: "Our lessons in the school room — in the parlour — at the table — our music, dancing, eating, drinking, working, playing, all are helps or hindrances to our improvement."[30] The typical family breakfast was described by Lane: "Each has a small red napkin or D'Oyley, in the lap, and the water, unleavened bread, apples and potatoes are handed round by one who is Ganymede on the occasion." And the main course of this spare early morning ritual was "conversation on some domestic Pythagorean topic."[31]

Alcott lived — and during this period wanted others to live — on the edge of choice, forcing all of life into the moral dimension by considering the virtue of every act. Food was a steady source of such good and evil, three times a day. Nor did dietary morality reside merely in such crude dichotomies as meat and vegetable; conscience might also banquet on the different degrees of spirituality in a pear or parsnip. Plants were better to eat than animals, and there was a hierarchy of goodness in plants themselves — "fruits take their place at the top, the grains next, then the herbs, last and lowest the roots."[32] These rigors seem a self-indulgence as much as a self-denial, a reveling in the moral universe. Alcott's strivings often seem to arise less out of cosmic idealism than cosmic vanity. As Emerson said, "Temperance that knows itself is not temperance, when it peaks and pines, and knows all it renounces."[33]

3. Abstinence and Insatiability

Alcott's desire to be better than his neighbors was part of a still more grandiose ambition to save the world by martyring himself. This masochistic egotism is displayed in his journals most boldly. Whereas Emerson's journal is a storehouse, and Thoreau's a proving ground, Alcott's is a case history. He regularly refers to it as a diary, while Emerson and Thoreau call theirs journals. Sometimes he seemed to think of it as a new gospel. "The miracle is in my thoughts and deeds," said he. "Let another write."[34] He kept the record, that was all. "It includes hints of my inmost doings and endeavorings, and is a psychological Diary for the time which it embraces. No important thought, emotion, or purpose has transpired in me that has not been noted therein. I have spoken of myself as of a second party. I have unveiled myself without the least attempt at concealment. This book has been my confessional, and I have enjoyed the times when I approached its pages."[35] He spoke once of the pleasure he got from reading his back pages — "I live over myself"[36] — and by the time he had finished the fiftieth volume, with thirty years of life still ahead of him, his diary was

> . . . taking the best of my time; and if it would take the best of me, and get an autobiography out of me, or help edit one, I should be content, and thank heaven for the performance. But I am not delivered so easily. Perhaps a Diary is the most difficult feat of authorship. I should be too happy if I had

before me the transcript of a single day. But the best refuses to be put into the pillory of words, and to be gazed at, as multitudes stare at culprits, and mock, in the market-places. I can't help writing, nevertheless, criminal as it seems to ink the mind in this manner. I write, write, driven by the demon with the quill behind his ear — eloquent of a morning, always, in praise of ink; then tempting me of afternoons to silence and depose him, as Luther did, by dashing the contents of my standish into his face for riddance of him once and forever.[37]

Thoreau once punned in his own journal, "Every sentence is the result of a long probation,"[38] but here sentences are literally punishments, Alcott appears again as culprit, and we are reminded of his skulking in the butcher's shop. Vanity and guilt are kept oscillating, and he seems rarely able to break out of the circle into the realm of other men and their reality.

Yet it was no petty self-enthrallment that Alcott suffered. The dimensions were as large as the moral universe. "A pretty kettle of fish we have here," Emerson said, "men of this vast ambition, who wish an ethics commensurate with nature, who sit expectant to be challenged to great performances, and are left without any distinct aim; there are openings only in the heavens before them, but no star which they approach; they have an invincible persuasion that the Right is to come to them in the social form, but they are aghast & desolate to know that they have no superiors in society. Society . . . proffers to these holy angels wishing to save the world, some bead or button of Communism, an Antislavery Cause, Prison Discipline, or Magdalen Refuge, or some other absorbent to suck his vitals into some one or another bitter partiality, & anyhow to deprive him of that essential condition which he prays for, adequateness."[39] Alcott tinkered with such causes at Fruitlands, and in the end when he had to face the failure of his great experiment in diet, education, family, community, and spirit, he merely turned the wheel one more notch, and indulged himself in the most extraordinary feat of self-denial of his life. He took to his bed and refused all food for three days, intending to starve himself to death. In later years he sometimes "reproached myself almost that in the fearfullest extreme of destitution at Fruitlands I did not persist in my purpose of passing beyond the need of animal support, my three day's abstinence from food having [brought me?] to near the final transit." He would have persisted, "had not the calls of Humanity detained me here yet longer, to defend these callow natures yet a while from the calamities of the social state till they should find a strength and clothing."[40] Only his family, Alcott would have us believe, could persuade him to give up this attempt at total abstinence. But "coming back" to his family had a certain additional appeal to a man of Alcott's temperament, since it entailed new sacrifices — giving up the larger consociate family, for one thing, and the communal board spread only with pure food, for another. Self-denial had to become once again a solitary pursuit — not an altogether unacceptable martyrdom.

Alcott's way was to make every act a matter for discipline and decision, whether reading or writing or eating or dying. "The thought he would record is something," Emerson noted shrewdly, "but the place, the page, the book, in which it is to be written are something also, not less than the proposition, so that usually in the attention to the marshalling, the thing marshalled dwindles & disappears."[41] One could not say the same thing of Thoreau. He was equally self-conscious — even sharper eyed and eared when it came to some areas of life — but he did not find every breath an excuse to consult the holy spirit. He strung his own moral sense tight enough, when he proposed in his journals, "Who knows how incessant a surveillance a strong man may maintain over himself, — how far subject passion and appetite to reason, and lead the life his imagination paints? . . . By a strong effort may he not command even his brute body in unconscious moments?"[42] At first glance this sort of inquisition would seem to suggest Alcott more than Thoreau, for it was the former whose "rigid asceticism" (Emerson's phrase) was then so well known. Both men were selfregarders, but Thoreau's surveillance over himself had more scrutiny and less scrupulosity. It was the difference between conscience and consciousness. Though he pursued and formulated his life to a most shocking degree, Thoreau never quite fingered it the way Alcott did.

In March 1845, when the Walden adventure was about to begin, Ellery Channing wrote to Thoreau: "I see nothing for you in this earth but that field which I once christened 'Briars'; go out upon that, build yourself a hut, & there begin the grand process of devouring yourself alive. I see no alternative, no other hope for you. Eat yourself up; you will eat nobody else, nor anything else."[43] It is possible to fast more absolutely, more voraciously, than to feed. Franz Kafka, himself a vegetarian, noted the fact: "The most insatiable people are certain ascetics, who go on hunger-strike in all spheres of life. . . ."[44] If Alcott was a kind of Bartleby trying to starve himself and thus achieve his punishment and escape his prison, Thoreau was a "hunger artist" who chose his prison, and whose fast was an excuse to turn inward on himself, that he might discover his own "vitals" and convert them to art. "He is the true artist," Thoreau wrote, "whose life is his material."[45]

The chapter of *Walden* called "Economy" is understandably concerned with food, since Thoreau reckoned it, along with shelter, clothing, and fuel, as making up the necessaries of existence. Why a chapter called "Higher Laws" should also be devoted in large part to diet might not be so apparent, without the backdrop of Alcott's experiments in purity. The chapter opens with food — fish and game. "As I came home through the woods with my string of fish, trailing my pole, it being now quite dark, I caught a glimpse of a woodchuck stealing across my path, and felt a strange thrill of savage delight, and was strongly tempted to seize and devour him raw. . . ."[46] This fine moment is to illustrate a pair of principles that Thoreau wants to discuss — "an instinct toward a higher, or, as it is named, spiritual life" and "another toward a primitive rank and savage one." Thoreau claims to "love" and "reverence" these instincts equally, though his chapter is in praise of the former.

Especially interesting, in contrast to Alcott, is the way in which Thoreau arrives at these "higher laws." Alcott's principles grew out of his relations with humanity, social and moral. Even after the failure of Fruitlands, his self-denials always had a public aspect, no matter how lacking of an audience. Thoreau's experiments with diet, woodchucks or Indian corn, were privately undertaken — in the forest, even in the dead of night. He cultivated his own instincts, consulted no other authorities. "As for these communities," he wrote in his journal at the beginning of Brook Farm, "I think I had rather keep bachelor's hall in hell than go to board in heaven. Do you think your virtue will be boarded with you? It will never live on the interest of your money, depend on it. The boarder has no home. In heaven I hope to bake my own bread and clean my own linen."[47]

If one asked just what seemed the advantage of eating alone, Emerson's answer would do: "All the fine aperçus are for individualism. The Spartan broth, the hermit's cell, the lonely farmer's life are poetic; the Phalanstery, the 'self supporting Village' (Owen) are culinary & mean."[48] Thoreau made the same point more personally — the "higher or poetic faculties" could best be preserved by abstaining "from animal food, and from much food of any kind."[49] He seems even to have regarded the material sustenance of food as a possible obstacle to the higher nourishment that might be drawn from it. A passage in his journal amplifies the hints of "Higher Laws":

> I have felt, when partaking of this inspiring diet, that my appetite was an indifferent consideration; that eating became a sacrament, a method of communion, an ecstatic exercise, a mingling of bloods, and sitting at the communion table of the world; and so have not only quenched my thirst at the spring but the health of the universe.
>
> The indecent haste and grossness with which our food is swallowed have cast a disgrace on the very act of eating itself. But I do believe that, if this process were rightly conducted, its aspect and effects would be wholly changed, and we

should receive our daily life and health, Antæus-like, with an ecstatic delight, and, with upright front, an innocent and graceful behavior, take our strength from day to day. This fragrance of the apple in my pocket has, I confess, deterred me from eating of it. I am more effectually fed by it another way.[50]

Perry Miller quotes another stray scrap of journal, probably of about the same date (1845), that fills out still more of the picture:

> What though my walk is [word obscure] and I do not find employment which satisfies my hunger & thirst, and the bee probing the thistle & loading himself with honey & wax seems better employed than I, my idleness is better than his industry. I would rather that my spirit hunger & thirst than that it forget its own wants in satisfying the hunger & thirst of the body.
>
> I would fain hunger & thirst after life forever & rise from the present enjoyment unsatisfied. I feel the necessity of treating myself with more respect than I have done — of washing myself more religiously in the ponds & streams if only for a symbol of our inward cleansing & refreshment — of eating and drinking more abstemiously and with more discrimination of savors — recruiting myself for new and worthier labor. There are certain things which only senses refined and purified may take cognizance of — May such senses be mine![51]

Far more explicitly than Alcott, Thoreau draws connections between his diet and his journal. Both are means only, toward that "incessant surveillance a strong man may maintain over himself." It is not even so much to live "the life that imagination paints" as it is to live exclusively in and through the imagination. Diet is to be "inspiring," even bathing is "only for a symbol." The imagination becomes a means of escape from "a cheap and superficial life," since "the trivial affairs of men" can be converted thereby into something "unstained and aloof."[52]

If Apollo must spend his time in the service of King Admetus, as Thoreau almost obsessively affirmed, it is still in his power to transmute that bondage into poetry. The "refining" and "purifying" of the senses is not really to sharpen spiritual perception; what is purified and refined is experience itself, so that eating becomes "a sacrament, and method of communion." Life is to be entirely constituted of symbolic acts, valued for their transcendental meaning alone. "Ah! if I could so live that there should be no desultory moment in all my life! that in the trivial season, when small fruits are ripe, my fruits might be ripe also!"[53] Of course it is Thoreau's journals where the harvest must be gathered in.

In these passages Thoreau approaches Alcott's burdening every circumstance with moral ponderance. In the long run he knew better. He criticized the vice in himself: "What offends me most in my compositions is the moral element in them. The repentant say never a brave word. Their resolves should be mumbled in silence. Strictly speaking, morality is not healthy."[54] Yet however much he may have tried to suppress it, the habit is everywhere evident in his writings, if not with the Alcottian moral tinge, then with the giddy intensity of manner that comes with never having quite enough to eat. It is with a sense of relief, of coming down from the thin air of the mountain tops, that one turns from both Thoreau and Alcott to their admiring critic Emerson, who had this to say of researches such as theirs: "A man cannot free himself by any selfdenying ordinances, neither by water nor potatoes, nor by violent passivities, by refusing to swear, refusing to pay taxes, by going to jail, or by taking another's crop or squatting on his land — By none of these ways can he free himself; no nor by paying his debts with money; only by obedience to his own genius; only by the freest activity in the way constitutional to him, does an angel seem to rise & lead him by the hand out of all wards of the prison."[55] This is a partial judgment, of course, and open to the question, "free for what?" Emerson's friends did not always agree with him in their notions of freedom and prison. Still, even for their purposes it seems a fair criticism. Self-denial was surely an artificial spur to conscience or consciousness. Suppose it were true that such virtues came into their sharpest focus only when a man's ordinary needs and satisfactions were balked; there was something perverse about setting up such tests and inhibitions solely to provoke these ecstasies of spirit.

4. Cannibalism and Appetite

Whatever abstemious impulses Emerson had, manifested themselves in his journal rather than the menu, so his dinners never suffered in their reputation for variety and plenty. Indeed, it is as hard to imagine him refusing a portion or inverting his glass as it is to think of him as incurious about the rest of nature's fare. He took note of the first appearance of seasonal foods on the table, much as Thoreau catalogued the first flowers or birds. Emersonian hospitality was proverbial. Thus Charles Lane was careful to avoid the Emerson house at mealtime, and Emerson was happy enough with that arrangement. Georgiana Bruce Kirby, who had been an early Brook Farmer, tells a marvelous Thanksgiving Day anecdote she heard there, about how Emerson had debated "with himself the question of inviting or not inviting his new friend to the festive board. To invite Mr. L. to America, and exclude him from his Thanksgiving table, would be both inhospitable and ungentlemanly; but then he was sure to spoil the dinner and destroy the appetite of his guests by assailing the turkey as the flesh of a dead animal, and by inviting attention to the fungi baked in the fermented bread, and to the alcohol in the wine which could never assimilate with the blood and tissues."[56] The upshot, according to Georgiana's informant, was one less place at dinner. Alcott, on the other hand, suffered through more than one hearty meal at the Emerson table. Once, another story goes, "the host is said to have dilated at considerable length, while carving a roast, upon the horrors of cannibalism. Bronson Alcott's face was working with amusement and barely suppressed glee until he suddenly burst forth with 'But Mr. Emerson, if we are to eat meat at all why should we *not* eat the *best*?'"[57] The anecdote is a good one because it brings out an element in vegetarianism that helps explain its appeal for Alcott and unattractiveness for Emerson. Alcott's joke is possible by virtue of the easy assumption that to abstain from meat is a civilized act, to eat it, savage. But of course this is not true. Taboos against meat-eating tend to go with cannibalism, and are much more common among primitives than civilized men. What is strictly a phenomenon of "higher" cultures is the decision of a single man, uninfluenced by law or custom, to abstain from flesh. And even this self-imposed taboo probably operates in much the same way as the more primitive variety — that is, as a means of coping with extreme ambivalence.

In any case Freud's dictum in *Totem and Taboo* applies: "what nobody desires to do does not have to be forbidden, and certainly whatever is expressly forbidden must be an object of desire."[58] The point, Emerson seemed to think, was the quality of that desire and its suppression. He too, as early as 1839, had defined the problem of diet as a matter of what was "agreeable to the imagination,"[59] but he went on to locate the responsibility for good digestion in the imagination itself and not its provender. "It makes no difference what a saintly soul eats or drinks; let him eat venison or roots, let him drink champagne or water, nothing will harm him or intoxicate or impoverish him: he eats as though he eat not, & drinks as though he drank not. But we are Skeptics over our dinner table & therefore our food is noxious & our bodies fat or lean. Looking as we do at means, & not at grand ends, being in our action disunited, our bodies have come to be detached also from our souls, & we speak of our health."[60] It was not only unnecessary to proscribe flesh, it was a self-defeating therapy, since it was not meat that was in question in the first place, nor health, but how to achieve their irrelevance. "The man is yet to arise who eats angels' food; who, working for universal aims, finds himself fed, he knows not how, & clothed he knows not how, & yet it is done by his own hands."[61]

Emerson could appreciate the "certain good effects not easily estimated" that came with the "least habit of dominion over the palate," but in the next breath he felt obliged to announce that he would not "be driven into a quiddling abstemiousness."[62] He regarded the establishment of "special diet," whatever its ingredients, as "superstition." All this goes to separate him from his insatiable friends, who not only ate "better" than their neighbors, but for whom no food was quite good enough. One may see the same distinction in his journals. Where Alcott and Thoreau seem always at work on themselves, the one fingering, the other digesting, Emerson rarely turns his attention inward in this way. It is a question whether his lack of self-consciousness is cause or result of the ease with which he composes, but surely the two are linked, just as his friends' great concern with self, as conscience or consciousness, went with a sense of hindrance and difficulty in writing. "I wish I could write as I feel and think," said Alcott over and over.[63] Thoreau seldom wasted time saying it, but here is a revealing exception: "But what does all this scribbling amount to? What is now scribbled in the heat of the moment one can contemplate with somewhat of satisfaction, but alas! to-morrow — aye, to-night — it is stale, flat, and unprofitable . . . . What may a man do and not be ashamed of it? . . . Can he not, wriggling, screwing, self-exhorting, self-constraining, wriggle or screw out something that shall live, — respected, intact, intangible, not to be sneezed at?"[64] The double seal of self-consciousness, unnecessary though it is, Thoreau placed in the margin, where he wrote "Carlyleish" against his thought. For a comparable passage in Emerson, one is reduced to that already quoted, in which he speaks of "this languid trick that we have gradually fallen into of writing & writing without end. After a day of humiliation &

stripes if I can write it down I am straightway relieved & can sleep well. After a day of joy the beating heart is calmed again by the diary. If grace is given me by all angels & I pray, if then I can catch one ejaculation of humility or hope & set it down in syllables, devotion is at an end."[65] Emerson is afraid of being too easily seduced and comforted by his journal; his friends worry that words seem inadequate to their visions.

In the context of diet and its evidence, there is some temptation to turn these complaints around on their authors, and wonder whether Emerson is not open to the accusation of a secret squeamishness, vanquished by fluency, and Thoreau and Alcott to the charge of courting obstacles, for the sake of being thrown back on themselves. The anecdote of Emerson's urbane remarks on cannibalism while carving the roast is relevant. For a while in the 1830s he seemed curiously interested in cannibalism, making several notes in his journal to the effect that men still could be found who ate their fellows. Nothing came of these entries however, and one is left feeling a bit cheated, as often with Emerson. He is willing to entertain any subject, taste any morsel, so long as no one asks him to consider his own digestion. His son reported: "Mr. Emerson ate what was set before him with natural appetite. . . . If he spoke of a dish it was to praise it in an amusing manner, never to find fault with it. . . . Discussions on the digestibility of food, he promptly suppressed, and if its composition was mentioned, he broke in with 'Oh no! it is made of roses,' or 'It is a beautiful crystallization.'"[66] Much of this reluctance is present in his journals, too. Not that he is never analytic in them, for he often is, but he is not so anxious to pursue problems as he is to discover solutions, and he is especially uninterested in what might be called "his own" problems. "If I should write an honest diary what should I say?" he once asked.[67] "I should not dare to tell all my story," he began another time.[68] Yet even these openings are to false trails — they lead into quite impersonal reports of matters that needed no such preface.

Why Emerson should be so reticent, especially in his journal, has puzzled posterity. If he ever harbored a private feeling, one could scarcely discover it from reading this record of his daily thoughts. His interest in his own consciousness seems entirely philosophical. Used to a later and more confessional form of journal-keeping, modern readers have thought him a cold fish. Even when he does manage to lay a transcended grief before us, as in the essay "Experience" where he speaks of his son's death, we have merely found our opinion confirmed. We want him to let his hair down, and are not satisfied with his effort to be honest and record his feelings without display or self-indulgence. It seems inhuman that he never gives way to passion or despair.

Emerson had heard about a kind of "experimental writing" — what today we would call "free association" or "automatic writing" — in which the author merely let his mind and pen wander "with a view to take what might fall, if any wit should transpire in all the waste pages."[69] At the time of Waldo's death, he found himself with his journal open, waiting for some solace or lesson from this source. "I in my dark hours may scratch the page if perchance any hour of recent life may project a hand from the darkness & inscribe a record." The "experiment" was a failure. No hand lurked in the darkness, and Emerson was left with this formulation: "Truth is our only armor in all passages of life & death." Although on another occasion he might accuse himself of using writing as an anodyne, his journal keeping was no comfort at this crisis. Writing was not unlike the rest of life — "writing & writing without end." When he found himself totally at a loss, the journal showed that only by its silence.

His personal reticence is not to be blamed or lamented, for it was as a sail to his ease and copiousness, the generosity of thought that he also possessed. Whatever the hidden dynamics of these exclusions, the return in literary production was very great, both in quantity and quality. There is a suppressed ambivalence in some of his work, but he does not stop to consider motives or to plaster over inconsistencies. He puts his full force behind a notion. One does not find him musing or debating with himself. Because there are few qualifications or defensive concessions, the journals are full of later retractions and second thoughts. Often a position may only be established over a period of years, and all the conflicting arguments may never be given any final expression. This gradual oscillating approach can be infuriating. How can a wise man entertain such contradictory views on a serious matter! It is carving the roast and speaking of the "horrors" of cannibalism. The glib insensitivity must protect some deep vulnerability. Or, to put it more generously, he could live with ambiguity; he could compound with the grim facts of life and had an appetite for truth however it served him. "I can reason down or at least deny every thing except this perpetual belly," he admitted one day. "Feed he must, & will, and I cannot make him respectable."[70] Keeping in mind the finicky sifting and sorting of Thoreau and Alcott, it does one good to see how little waste there was in Emerson's art. He cleaned his plate, as it were. The revisions are very few, and the proportion of material finally used in lectures and essays is incredibly high. His mind did not catch and snag on every alternative thought or phrase, but followed with healthy confidence to the end of each inspiration wherever it might lead. Not so Thoreau or Alcott — nor, one sometimes suspects, would they have it so.

Thoreau's willingness to trust his instincts for his principles could lead him into inconsistency too. But rather than wait it out, he would soar above the impasse on wings of paradox. The whole chapter on "Higher Laws" for example, is nothing more than Thoreau plundering his own mixed feelings about diet. "Once or twice . . . I found myself ranging the woods, like a half-starved hound, with a strange abandonment, seeking some kind of venison which I might devour, and no morsel could have been too savage for me."[71] Somehow by the end of the chapter this wildness and "strange abandonment" is transmuted into "sensuality" and is opposed to purity and chastity. There are similar gulfs of sensibility between his boast that he could "eat a fried rat with a good relish, if it were necessary," and his "wonder" in the very next paragraph "how you and I, can live this slimy beastly life, eating and drinking."[72] Because there is scarcely any blurring or false synthesizing, as when Alcott is playing with his ambivalency, Thoreau's range of feeling is much greater. This swing of affect tempts a reader to think more seriously about Thoreau's casual reference to cannibalism: "Whatever my own practice may be, I have no doubt that it is a part of the destiny of the human race, in its gradual improvement, to leave off eating animals, as surely as the savage tribes have left off eating each other when they came in contact with the more civilized."[73] (Would it be useful to think of the woodchuck as Thoreau's totem?)

At the very least, it is certain that Thoreau's trials of diet were more searching and more daring than Alcott's, not merely a matter of abstention or self-justification, but also of exploration and perhaps even transgression. If taboo has to do with inexplicable yet inviolable law, then Thoreau was interested in it and its grounding in spiritual nature. What were the "higher laws" if not such sacred prohibitions? Alcott was concerned with ethical law — what one can choose not to do — while Thoreau was chiefly fascinated with these "higher laws" by which one is bound whatever one may choose. He is interested not only in righteous acts, but also in the price paid for sin and sacrilege, the terms on which one has one's life and nature. Alcott feels his way along the edge of will and duty, Thoreau plunges into the conditions of existence.

Either investigation involved finding limits to batter against. Getting life into a corner meant getting oneself into a corner — a hut, a journal. It meant, to an extent, failure — for consciousness is a product of hindrance and deferred action. One might court failure, as Henry Adams seemed to do, for the sake of the compensations of will and consciousness, or one might institute "selfdenying ordinances" like Alcott and

Thoreau, to make both success and failure superfluous. The victory over the self is always a defeat as well, so that the needs of both consciousness and ambition are served. After such tastes and habits were established, continuous monitoring might seem necessary to prove one's existence. Every passage of life would be in danger of fading into meaningless oblivion if not rescued by an effort of the conscious will. Thoreau viewed his journal as a net for "those thoughts and impressions which I am most liable to forget that I have had; which would have in one sense the greatest remoteness, in another, the greatest nearness to me."[74] The ambition is to get everything into his journal, under his control. Emerson once said of him, "H.'s conversation consisted of a continual coining of the present moment into a sentence & offering it to me. I compared it to a boy who from the universal snow lying on the earth gathers up a little in his hand, rolls it into a ball, & flings it at me."[75] But the snow kept melting, the present moments went skidding into the past, and no imagination could keep up. In spite of Ellery Channing, no one could totally devour himself.

"New Modes of Thinking"

I am my own man more than most men, yet the loss of a few persons would be most impoverishing. . . . It were too much to say that the Platonic world I might have learned to treat as cloud-land, had I not known Alcott, who is a native of that country, yet I will say that he makes it as solid as Massachusetts to me; and Thoreau gives me, in flesh & blood & pertinacious Saxon belief, my own ethics.

Emerson's *Journals*

What then was the significance of all these feats of self-denial and abnegation? How could it help America for an intellectual to withdraw from society, despise all labor but self-sufficient farming, abstain from meat, refuse his taxes, decline even to engage in utopian alternatives, live alone in a hut in the woods, and cultivate his consciousness?

It is tempting to see the transcendentalists with modern eyes, as part of a counterculture movement like that of recent times, the first to be disgusted with the commercialism that led Emerson to say the "very savage on the shores of the N. W. America, holds up his shell & cries 'a dollar!'"[1] Elements of the "new consciousness" of the 1840s can be found in modern notions of an "alternative life-style." Many of the differences are only a matter of urgency, and to some extent despair. The agrarian impulse is now colored by a sense of the precariousness of the planet's ecosystem. The desire to find meaningful, self-justifying kinds of work is all the more pressing in the context of automation, bureaucratic office work, and unemployment. The revulsion from a corrupt world of business and trade has spread to include much else in our social institutions, in proportion to the degree that these too have become mere commodities, bought and sold on the market.

In these concluding pages I want to consider some of our responses to these modern facts of life in the light of the transcendentalist experience. I am not primarily concerned with the problems of our society — who cannot recite them? — but with the kinds of solutions we think of applying, our attempts to deal with our plight.

There is probably no part of contemporary American society that values eloquence in the way that almost everyone did in the middle of the last century. The blame for this loss can be divided, I suppose, between the lying politicians and the babbling media. It is no longer possible — if it ever was — to accuse the establishment alone of this double-talk; both tendencies, manipulative and publicist, infected the "movement" during the 1960s. The exceptions remind us of our loss. A few famous speeches and public statements of dissent seemed authentic in an old-fashioned way. Typically these moved thousands. One thinks of Mario Savio's urging the students at Berkeley "to put your bodies upon the gears and upon the wheels" of the academic "machine," or Martin Luther King's "I have a dream." Significant as these moments may have been, however, it was the poets and songwriters who gave the movement its slogans and slang — "we shall not be moved," "weathermen," and so on — and Beatnik lingo became a badge of solidarity.

Given the opportunity to address a vast audience of energetic reformers, intellectuals raced to produce tracts of social criticism, some of it quite forceful. But affluence and commercialism obscure the impact of such books, and neither sales nor media fame is a trustworthy measure of influence. For example, everybody bought a copy of *Growing Up Absurd*, and many activists agreed that Paul Goodman's ideas were crucial to their own views; yet it is astonishing to discover how few, leaders or rank and file, actually read the book they all had on the shelf and, in a sense, "knew by heart." Ideas were in the air, but rhetoric was not trusted and arguments counted for less than acts. "Don't trust anyone over 30" was a shibboleth that really meant "Don't believe anything you read." In the long run this attitude fostered demagoguery rather than prophetic wisdom. Voices comparable to Emerson's or Thoreau's did not emerge, for there was really no one to listen. Goodman, the likeliest candidate, gave up and turned to poetry and philosophy, very much in the transcendentalist mode, but as he did so he lost his larger audience. In the 1970s his name is rarely heard. What a contrast to Emerson's latter-day fame!

The deep distrust of public speech has had as one corollary the creation of another form of assertion, comparable to and (through Gandhi) a direct outgrowth of the vigorous dissent of Thoreau, Alcott, and other nay-sayers of the mid-nineteenth century. When they quoted him in the 1960s, few radicals knew the complicated way that Thoreau had come to his own civil disobedience, but they were right that it was his tradition (as well as that of William Lloyd Garrison, Henry Clarke Wright, and the nonresistant wing of abolitionism) that led to our sit-ins and demonstrations. Not only were the techniques of Christian nonviolence similar, but the very causes, pacifism and civil rights for blacks, were the same.

There have been fewer dramatic instances of civil disobedience in the 1970s, although some of the demonstrations against nuclear power have matched the classic cases of the 1960s; but at the same time it seems likely that the potential for such responses to authority has increased enormously, simply by virtue of widespread familiarity with the techniques — and successes — of nonviolent direct action. In a world where most public speech is not to be trusted, propaganda by the deed may be the only possible political eloquence. Americans are still among the most docile and governable citizens in the world, so that even their protests and refusals are typically framed as civil acts ("civil disobedience" in two senses), but respect for authority is breaking down — with what ultimate consequences for the polity no one knows.

At least one exception to this overall distrust and denial ought to be mentioned, particularly since it resembles a transcendentalist phenomenon rather closely. The 1960s gave rise to a multitude of activist periodicals, from the standard-bearers like *Liberation* and *New Left Notes* to the counterculture emporiums like *Rolling Stone* and *The Whole Earth Catalogue*. Many of these have folded, and even those that took their places have folded, yet radical intellectuals continue to search for some means of addressing a dispersed and amorphous constituency. For the most part the new voices are mere echoes of the 1960s; however, there have been some examples of a very different kind that remind one of the call of Bronson Alcott for a new sort of private discourse, epistles and diaries and conversations. These irregular publications are all very unpretentious, cheaply printed or mimeographed, homemade jobs. Often a single issue is all that sees the light. Their subjects tend to be ecology or life-style, with titles like *Simple Living, Plowshares,* or *The Soil of Liberty*; more important are their writers, professionals at neither writing nor radicalism, but more or less ordinary people who have had some rousing experience in life, tested some idea or undergone some transformation which they want to share with a reader. These accounts, always profoundly autobiographical, may tell how an engineer quit his job and turned to making oboes for a living, how a parent dealt with his seven-year-old's consumerism, how a senior citizen learned to ride a tricycle, or any of dozens of stories that report some similar lesson. In the very nature of the case these little periodicals often close up shop after the first issue, for there is nothing further to be said until more life has been lived. Also in the nature of the case, it is hard to know how to assess the phenomenon: how many such publications are there? what impulse do they represent? what is their effect? Are they perhaps examples of "new modes of thinking," a modern transcendentalist testimony? They scarcely represent a formidable challenge to the "media" or to the "system," if one takes these as the opponents to be confronted and displaced. But then Thoreau's little autobiographical account of his night in jail was not much of a threat to the government that made war on Mexico and policed slavery. And who cares if a man goes off to live alone in the woods for a couple of years?

It might be answered that Thoreau was a very great writer, who turned his experience into art. No doubt, but the transcendentalist position was this: whatever one's gifts, true eloquence arises in personal experience reported with absolute candor, if only in one's diary. "Only what is private, & yours, & essential, should ever be printed or spoken," said Emerson, and Thoreau began *Walden* by explaining that "I, on my side, require of every writer, first or last, a simple and sincere account of his own life."[2] I am not saying that we should be listening for the voice of some new Emerson or Thoreau — rather, as they would have said, for the voice of humanity.

The transcendentalists' first question was not how to write or speak, but how to live. If one answered that, eloquence would follow. How to live: how to make a living, where to live, whether to live with others or alone.

"Simplicity!" cried Thoreau, hoping to pare existence down to its essentials; but his shack at the pond was crowded with contingencies nonetheless. Struggle as they did to arrive at principles, the transcendentalists' answers had the inconsistency as well as the solidity of practical experience. Yet if we take the long view, comparing their thoughts and acts over the years, we can see a pattern emerging. The transcendentalists believed in organic values, they admired the institutions that seemed given in nature and the species. Thus they were inveterately domestic, rooted to place and heritage; home and family determined much, and the larger community was implied by neighborhood and kinship rather than by the abstractions of politics. Work was similarly founded in these primary conditions: as much as possible, one's living was to be harvested from the soil of one's own tilling; the easy riches of trade and the division of labor were viewed as the snares of economists, theoreticians who understood arithmetic better than the requirements of the spirit. The test was Thoreau's "Do what nobody else can do for you. Omit to do anything else."[3] Accordingly, government and corporate power were regarded as encroachments not only on freedom but more importantly on the balance of needs and competencies. Citizens ought to exercise their powers where they would authentically reach, in family and neighborhood, no further. The same principle applied to the resistance to evil, whether in the form of the devil or the state. Civil disobedience was a choice one could make in good conscience only on one's own ground.

Much of this program sounds conventionally American, the traditional position of individualism. Yet it is very far from the current facts of life in the United States. Families are no longer the large, multi-generational institutions Thoreau and Emerson lived in, neighborhoods are mere suburban grids, no one grows his own food or even knows where it comes from. Work is universally despised, especially manual labor. The competence of an individual is thought to lie in special training and skills rather than self-sufficiency or character. Everything is measured in dollars and time. Words like "spirit" and "soul" are slang expressions for the commodities of entertainment. Government and corporate power, while mistrusted, are called upon to make all public decisions, enforce morality and justice, and provide the goods of life.

This is scarcely the individualism advocated by the transcendentalists, and Emerson would be just as accurate today as he was in 1848 when he said, "Individualism has never been tried. All history, all poetry deal with it only & because now it was in the minds of men to go alone and now before it was tried, now, when a few began to think of the celestial Enterprise, sounds this tin trumpet of a French Phalanstery and the newsboys throw up their caps & cry, Egotism is exploded; now for Communism! But all that is valuable in the Phalanstery comes of individualism. You may settle it in your hearts that when you get a great man, he will be hard to keep step with. Spoons & skimmers may well enough lie together, but vases & statues must have each its own pedestal."[4]

Of course such terms need interpretation. Emerson's "great man" was not always the touchstone, and the individualism of New England yeomanry appealed to him at least as much as the individualism of Napoleon or Goethe. Nor would he have respected the literal facts of our modern "private enterprise" or our media "heroes," individualistic as some people assume them to be; while on the other hand the communitist phenomena of the 1960s had virtues that he certainly would have admired: the libertarian stance, the antipathy to bureaucratic power, the reliance on techniques of direct action and nonviolence, and in the later stages of the movement the discovery of "counter-culture" values — voluntary poverty, homesteading, the cultivation of Taoist philosophy. Even the violent tactics of the weathermen might have gotten some sympathy from the admirers of John Brown.

But the transcendentalists would have found much to disturb them in these same attitudes and events. The emphasis on political activism, on organized groups working on a national scale to effect social change, would have reminded them of the reformers they mistrusted in the 1840s, especially as the modern movement began to fragment into parties and factions scrambling for power. "These have such gross & bloody chiefs to mislead them," said Emerson in 1848, "and are so full of hatred & murder, that the scholar recoils."[5]

All this is obvious. More interesting because more problematic is the question of how the transcendentalists would view the attempt to combine certain values they thought incompatible: family and community, homestead and trade, manual labor and the scholar's life. Particularly in the 1970s, as the counterculture has sifted itself down to those who are not merely slumming but permanently out of the mainstream, we can identify some lasting experiments and tendencies that would have surprised Emerson and Thoreau — though perhaps not Alcott, who, after all, was ready to found a utopian community where the family would be "consociate" and Orpheus happy at the plow. The surprise is not that communal ventures have proved viable, for there was plenty of evidence to that effect in the 1840s, but that they could coexist in the long run with family ties and the domestic virtues.

Probably the expectations of the transcendentalists were correct in the main, for it can be observed that those communities which have maintained the strictest communism are usually monastic in their other characteristics, whereas the experiments that have managed to integrate family life tend to be settlements and neighborhoods, with strong cooperative institutions, rather than single households comprising many members. And the single-household exceptions, appropriately enough, are often urban, where the communitists go off to work or school every day, gather as a group only for meals and business meetings, and take much of their leisure in family or individual units. Even with these safety valves and cooling systems, the rate of divorce and turnover seems likely to be higher in such establishments, as Charles Lane would have predicted.

The complicated combinations of homestead and trade are still more difficult to assess. As strict and self-sufficient a pair of vegetarians as Scott and Helen Nearing found it necessary to raise a cash crop, and the temptations of the roadside stand lead directly to tractors and bank loans. If you inquire into the trouble areas of any homesteading operation, they invariably appear along this roadside, the boundary line between what is necessary for subsistence and what is produced for sale. People work out their own solutions — like the Nearings' "no buying on credit" and "no work after the year's living is in." Sociologists as well as economists might learn a great deal from such rules of thumb, but so far not much is known about the possibilities of homesteading within our affluent/scarcity society.

On the compatibility of manual labor with intellectual work the transcendentalists had mixed views. It is easy to find testimony for either position — that physical exertion is beneficial to thought, or that it is not. Perhaps more relevant to modern concerns is the question, what *kind* of thought? And is the hindrance labor or the social intercourse that usually accompanies it? At Brook Farm Hawthorne found that both exhausted his imagination. Of the two, society proved the more dangerous: "I have not the sense of perfect seclusion, which has always been essential to my power of producing anything. It is true, nobody intrudes into my room; but still I cannot be quiet. Nothing here is settled — everything is but beginning to arrange itself. . . . My mind will not be abstracted."[6] It should be added that Hawthorne never had such difficulties once married and living with his family, for as Charles Lane pointed out, the nuclear family was merely another form of living in solitude, wife and children being felt as attributes of selfhood rather than separate consciousnesses which one had always to allow for.

The modern experience in communes seems to conform to these lessons, with some exceptions. Of the two, hard work probably tires the spirit less than communal life usurps it. But in either case, can it be so easily determined that the loss is serious? There are certainly too many books written and published, and even more unquestionably there is too much purely abstract thinking agitating people's minds. Alcott one day told Emerson he thought "Gardening . . . was a good refuge for reformers, Abolitionists, &c. that they might acquire that realism which we so approve in merchants and in Napoleon."[7] Emerson's own view was, "Better that the book should not be quite so good, and the bookmaker abler and better, and not himself a ludicrous contrast to all that he has written."[8] And Thoreau testified, "I find that whatever hindrances may occur I write just about the same amount of truth in my journal, for the record is more concentrated, and usually it is some very real and earnest life, after all, that interrupts."[9] If there is one universal defect in the thought of contemporary intellectuals, whether reformers or novelists or scholars, it is that not enough real and earnest life intrudes on their literary solitude.

It was to this issue, the virtues and vices of thinking and writing, that the transcendentalists kept returning, as an animal licks its wound. The "new modes of thinking" they claimed to have discovered were their solution to ambivalence and their apology for noncommitment. There were many reasons why they could not enter into "real and earnest life" in society, not unlike the reasons that a young person today hesitates to go into politics, business, or even the professions. How then to be justified in the world, without a worldly vocation? While communitists and other radicals proposed external reforms that seemed mere alterations of the facade, the transcendentalists asked for a revolution within, first of all within their own hearts. Thus they turned writing and thought on themselves in their journals, which like the old Puritan diaries were spiritual self-examinations with serious implications for salvation or damnation. Their entries were not only comments on life, considered after the event, but life itself, the event unfolding. Conversely, every authentic act of life was, as it were, an entry on a page, a thought formulated and recorded.

The result was indeed a new mode of thinking, with extraordinary effects. At their most characteristic and best, they succeeded in abolishing the difference between thought and act. Emerson said proudly of Alcott that he made the Platonic world "as solid as Massachusetts," while Thoreau "gives me, in flesh and blood and pertinacious Saxon belief, my own ethics."[10]

This achievement was not easy or complete. Alcott seems to manage it only in his conversation (and we must take Emerson's word for *that*). Emerson succeeded most of all in his journals, where he could miraculously open himself to inspiration and find words for every moment and feeling, so that one often has the experience he himself regarded as the quintessence of eloquence, when speaker and listener become one in the thought. (But Emerson rarely preserved this angelic power in his essays, though he lifted their paragraphs verbatim from his notebooks.) Thoreau had still another problem and another gift. His prose seldom reached the pure realm Emerson dwelt in; the labor he lavished on it made it glitter not ascend. Yet he had the ability Emerson and Alcott lacked of wholly identifying himself with his work, so that what he was and what he said became indistinguishable.

All three, but especially Thoreau, achieve what they do by virtue of fierce self-discipline and restraint. Journal writing can be a purifying spiritual exercise, and as we have seen in the preceding chapter there were other practices of abnegation that contributed like martial arts to meditation. Perhaps this is the aspect of their accomplishment that modern students find most alien and difficult to comprehend. Little in our experience prepares us for their program of refusals and abstinence, living as we do in unexampled plenty and limitless choice. Therefore this is the lesson we most need to learn from them.

They were among the first to confront the world as we know it — a world of *too much*, in which too many possibilities offer themselves, too many careers, too many possessions and pleasures, too much complexity and ramification, too much leisure in which to think about all these alternatives, and to dream up more. The result for us has been a crisis of faith and selfhood: we lose touch with our animal nature, the character of the species and its necessities, and we therefore lose touch with our desires, evolved to help us fill those needs, and useless without apparent hierarchy and constraints. We are full of will and anxiety, without anything to attach to. The transcendentalists sensed these dangers at the outset, and drew back horrified. The sense of glut revolted them, and they reacted violently. I do not think I overstate this, even for Emerson whose taste for experience was enormous. They deplored the breakdown of traditional values — land, kinship, hierarchy —

that de Tocqueville reports in *Democracy in America*, and they set about replacing these with transcendentalist values — which came to the same things, argued from new premises.

What Emerson so admired in Thoreau (his "own ethics") could also be seen in the oldest farmers in the area, as Emerson often noted. It was a narrower, simpler life in some ways, but a richer one in others. Although it no longer came naturally, as part of being introduced into the world, the transcendentalists thought that it might be forced, by pure will, into a hothouse bloom. This was Thoreau's intention in going out to Walden Pond, Alcott's at Fruitlands, Emerson's whenever he picked up his pen — to find the true inspiration by removing oneself from superfluities, society, distracting influences. A shack in the woods, or a summerhouse in the next field, was the ideal place to reestablish the organic rhythms and hierarchies. Depending on the individual, more and more abnegation might be needed to arrive at awareness, but however much, the direction was clear: voluntary poverty, abstention from the society's commodities and "standard of living," refusal to contribute to the general drift either by taxes or by other service — these threw one back upon oneself most absolutely. And for a writer like Thoreau they became subject matter as well as the conditions for writing at all, his new mode of thinking.

Whether or not we need any writers like Thoreau today (it is not exactly clear what we would use them for), we can profit by his example. People complain, as Lane seemed to in the 1840s, that Thoreau's model, or the myth it has become, leads his disciples astray — into withdrawal, self-involvement, and ostrichlike acquiescence in the abuses and injustices of society. But neither in his day nor in ours is his abstinence without political and social consequences of the profoundest kinds. Were it so, his acts and thoughts would never have influenced so many persons, some of very great character and influence themselves, like Gandhi and King.

Now more than ever we need to clear our shelves, rein in and restrict ourselves. We need to confront our fetishism of

things, our surfeit of advertising and media chatter, our out-
rageous ambitions. The transcendentalists asked for a change
of heart in all citizens, but first in themselves. We need to begin
where they did. Emerson pointed out in "Politics" that you
cannot legislate morality; it comes from the individuals who
act morally. Of course external conditions need to be changed,
and we know in part how they should be changed; it is important to discern precisely what things are amiss in society.
Inequities in the distribution of goods are merely part of the
larger problem that also includes how to humanize their production, and the deeper problem, how to moderate our greed.
These are moral as well as social matters, and cannot be solved
by arithmetic or wealth. There is no guarantee that the transcendentalist methods of self-denial and self-examination
would serve to take the place of traditional culture and religious
faith — they probably would not — but the new modes of
thinking we need are more likely to develop in an atmosphere
of revolutionary abstinence than in the welter of indulgence we
are used to. Perhaps our counterculture is a beginning in this
direction, even more for its withdrawal from the official media
culture and the "standard of living" than for its affirmation of
self-sufficiency and communal life. Another hopeful sign is the
general appeal of what have been called "consciousness-raising
groups." The women's movement especially has encouraged
new kinds of discourse, not so unlike the "conversations"
advocated by some of the transcendentalists. We need exchanges
like these to help dissolve the rigid distinctions between public
and private life.

For good or ill, there is little chance that Jefferson's
agrarian ideal will be realized in our lifetimes, with a sturdy,
autonomous yeomanry taking the place of industrial society
and agribusiness; on the other hand, examples of independence
need not be limited to homesteading, as food coops, home
workshops, and professional collectives demonstrate. Transcendentalist self-reliance and resistance to anonymous authority are virtues that may be practiced almost anywhere in our

culture. No "total" solution to our condition is in the offing, and we are right to mistrust medicines as merely new versions of our disease. We ought to cherish every sort of dissent from uniformity, whether radical or conservative. The examples of Emerson, Alcott, and Thoreau are not indispensable — any hard look at our society is enough to provoke the healthy revulsion called for — but let us turn to them nonetheless for what few others can give us, the inspiration of our own mythic heroes, men of flesh and blood, who first confronted the temptations and delusions of modern life and had the courage and good sense to say nay. If it is a change of heart that we most need, perhaps their example can inspire it.

Notes

Notes to Introduction

1. "Man the Reformer," *Nature, Addresses, and Lectures*, vol. 1 of *The Collected Works of Ralph Waldo Emerson*, ed. Robert E. Spiller and Alfred R. Ferguson (Cambridge, Mass., 1971-), 148. (Cited hereafter as Emerson's *Works*).

2. "Historic Notes of Life and Letters in New England," *The Complete Works of Ralph Waldo Emerson*, ed. Edward Waldo Emerson, 12 vols. (Boston and New York, 1903-1904), X, 329. (Cited hereafter as Emerson's *Works* 1903 edn.)

3. "Introductory Lecture," Emerson's *Works*, I, 181.

4. *The Journals and Miscellaneous Notebooks of Ralph Waldo Emerson*, ed. William H. Gilman, Alfred R. Ferguson, et al. (Cambridge, Mass., 1960-), X, 311.

5. Emerson's *Journals*, X, 318, 326.

6. "The Transcendentalist," Emerson's *Works*, I, 208.

7. Emerson's *Journals*, VIII, 38.

8. *Nature*, Emerson's *Works*, I, 45.

9. "The Transcendentalist," Emerson's *Works*, I, 212.

10. Charles Lane, "Social Tendencies," *The Dial*, 4 (1843), 197.

11. Emerson's *Journals*, IX, 446-47.

12. Ibid., VIII, 267.

13. *The Portable Melville*, ed. Jay Leyda (New York, 1952), p. 428.

Notes to "Eloquence Needs No Constable"

1. *Memoirs of Margaret Fuller Ossoli*, ed. R. W. Emerson et al., 2 vols. (Boston, 1852), II, 14.

2. Ibid., I, 107, 311.

3. "Days from a Diary." *The Dial*, 2 (1842), 43.

4. *The Journals of Bronson Alcott*, ed. Odell Shepard (Boston, 1938), pp. 102, 422.

5. *The Journals and Miscellaneous Notebooks of Ralph Waldo Emerson,* ed. William H. Gilman, Alfred R. Ferguson, et al. (Cambridge, Mass., 1960-), VIII, 181.

6. Alcott's *Journals*, p. 281.

7. *The Correspondence of Emerson and Carlyle*, ed. Joseph Slater (New York, 1964), p. 171.

8. Carl Bode, *The American Lyceum* (New York, 1956), pp. 49-50, 134.

9. *The Complete Works of Ralph Waldo Emerson*, ed. Edward Waldo Emerson, 12 vols. (Boston and New York, 1903-1904), VII, 372.

10. Emerson's *Journals*, IV, 335.

11. Ibid., V, 32.

12. Ibid., VII, 281.

13. Alcott's *Journals*, p. 225.

14. Emerson's *Journals*, XIII, 282.

15. Ibid., VII, 301.

16. Ibid., VII, 405.

17. Ibid., VII, 52.

18. Ibid., X, 357.

19. Ibid., V, 167.

20. Alcott's *Journals*, p. 76.

21. *The Plain Speaker*, 1 (1841), 26.

22. Emerson's *Journals*, VII, 177; *Walden*, ed. J. Lyndon Shanley (Princeton,N.J., 1971), pp. 268-269.

23. *The Letters of A. Bronson Alcott*, ed. Richard L. Herrnstadt (Ames, Iowa, 1969), p. 643.

24. Emerson's *Journals*, XIII, 38.

25. Ibid., VIII, 211; V, 10.

26. Ibid., VII, 41.

27. Ibid., VII, 539.

28. Ibid., XIV, 87.

29. Ibid., VIII, 271.

30. Ibid., XI, 19.

31. Ibid., XIV, 83.

32. Ibid., XIII, 183.

33. Ibid., VII, 347.

34. Ibid.

35. Ibid., XIII, 16.

36. Ibid., VIII, 118.

37. *The Correspondence of Henry David Thoreau*, ed. Walter Harding and Carl Bode (New York, 1958), p. 426.

38. *The Journal of Henry D. Thoreau*, ed. Bradford Torrey and Francis H. Allen, 14 vols. (Boston, 1906), III, 390. When Alcott and Channing were first getting acquainted, Alcott told Thoreau that, "if they were to live in the same house, they would soon sit with their backs to each other" (Thoreau's *Correspondence*, pp. 204-205).

39. Thoreau's *Correspondence*, p. 42.

40. Ibid., pp. 124-125. Margaret's "noble piece" was her feminist essay for *The Dial*, "The Great Lawsuit," later expanded (though folded no thicker) in the celebrated *Woman in the Nineteenth Century*.

41. Ibid., p. 251.

42. Perry Miller, *Consciousness in Concord* (Boston, 1958), p. 208.

43. Ibid., p. 199.

44. Thoreau's *Correspondence*, p. 260.

45. Thoreau's *Journal*, I, 143.

46. Emerson's *Journals*, VIII, 261.

47. Ibid., VII, 477.

48. Ibid., VIII, 253-54.

49. Ibid., VIII, 392.

50. Ibid., VIII, 367.

51. "Days from a Diary," p. 435.

52. *Walden*, p. 84.

53. Emerson's *Journals*, VIII, 367; *The Letters of Ralph Waldo Emerson*, ed. Ralph L. Rusk, 6 vols. (New York and London, 1939), III, 196, 214.

54. Thomas Wentworth Higginson, *Cheerful Yesterdays* (Boston, 1898), p. 158.

55. Emerson's *Journals*, XIII, 391.

56. Alcott's *Journals* p. 446.

57. Ibid., p. 272.

58. Ibid., p. 272n.

59. Walter Harding, "A Check List of Thoreau's Lectures," *Bulletin of the New York Public Library* (February 1948), p. 2.

60. Alcott's *Letters*, p. 53.

61. Alcott's *Journals*, p. 231; Channing's characterization of Alcott was in a letter to Elizabeth P. Peabody — see her *Reminiscences of Rev. Wm. Ellery Channing* (Boston, 1880), p. 414.

62. Thoreau's *Journal*, v, 365.

63. Alcott's *Journals*, p. 244.

64. Emerson's *Journals*, XI, 412.

65. Emerson's *Letters*, III, 339-40.

66. Thoreau's *Correspondence*, pp. 77-78.

67. Emerson's *Letters*, II, 335.

68. Letter from Charles Lane, "State Slavery — Imprisonment of A. Bronson Alcott — Dawn of Liberty," *Liberator*, 13, no. 4 (27 Jan. 1843), 16.

69. See Emerson's *Letters*, III, 230; Emerson's *Works* 1903 edn., X, 440.

70. Lane, "State Slavery . . . ," p. 16.
71. Alcott's *Journals*, p. 189.
72. Ibid., p. 179.
73. Ibid., pp. 183-84.
74. This passage, not printed in Odell Shepard's edition of Alcott's *Journals*, is quoted by the kind permission of Mrs. F. W. Pratt, and the Houghton Library of Harvard University, owners of the manuscript.
75. "Resistance to Civil Government," *Æsthetic Papers*. 1 (1849), 199-200.
76. Ibid., p. 190.
77. Alcott's *Journals*, p. 201.
78. "Resistance to Civil Government," p. 205.
79. Emerson's *Journals*, IX, 323.
80. "Resistance to Civil Government," p. 195.
81. Emerson's *Journals*, IX, 445.
82. Ibid., IX, 446.
83. Ibid., IX, 446-47.
84. *English Traits*, Emerson's *Works* 1903 edn., V, 286-87.
85. "Politics," Emerson's *Works* 1903 edn., III, 219-20.
86. Ibid., p. 221.
87. "War," *Æsthetic Papers*, (1849), 48-49. For Garrison's praise, see Emerson's *Works* 1903 edn., XI, 578.
88. Ibid., pp. 47-48.
89. "Resistance to Civil Government," pp. 201-202.
90. "Politics," Emerson's *Works* 1903 edn., III, 215-16, 220-21.
91. "Resistance to Civil Government," p. 195.
92. Ibid., p. 198.
93. Ibid., p. 199.
94. Emerson's *Journals*, IX, 446.
95. "Resistance to Civil Government," pp. 207-208.
96. Ibid., p. 210.
97. Emerson's *Journals*, IX, 267.
98. Ibid., IX, 390-91.
99. Ibid., IX, 434.
100. "Man the Reformer," *Nature, Addresses, and Lectures*, vol. 1 of *The Collected Works of Ralph Waldo Emerson*, ed. Robert E. Spiller and Alfred R. Ferguson (Cambridge, Mass., 1971-), 157.
101. Emerson's *Journals*, IX, 365.
102. *Consciousness in Concord*, p. 76.
103. Thoreau's *Journal*, III, 5.

Notes to "Huts Are Safe"

1. *The Letters of Ralph Waldo Emerson*, ed. Ralph L. Rusk, 6 vols. (New York and London, 1939), II, 322.

2. See Arthur Eugene Bestor, *Backwoods Utopias: The Sectarian and Owenite Phases of Communitarian Socialism in America: 1663-1829* (Philadelphia, 1950), p. 243, for a "statistical summary" of communities founded before 1860.

3. Quoted in O. B. Frothingham, *George Ripley* (Boston, 1882), pp. 307-308.

4. See L. F. Anderson, "The Manual Labor School Movement," *Educational Review*, 46 (1913), 369-86; John R. Commons and Associates, *History of Labour in the United States*, 2 vols. (New York, 1918), I, 248-49; George Ripley, "Pestalozzi," *The Christian Examiner*, 11 (1832), 347-73.

5. *The Journals and Miscellaneous Notebooks of Ralph Waldo Emerson*, ed. William H. Gilman, Alfred R. Ferguson, et al. (Cambridge, Mass., 1960-), VIII, 210.

6. Chandler Robbins, *The Disorders of Literary Men* (Boston, 1825).

7. Emerson's *Journals*, VII, 71.

8. Ibid., VII, 405.

9. Ibid., VII, 526.

10. "Man the Reformer," *Nature, Addresses, and Lectures*, vol. 1 of *The Collected Works of Ralph Waldo Emerson*, ed. Robert E. Spiller and Alfred R. Ferguson (Cambridge, Mass., 1971-), 147-48.

11. George Ripley, "Life in Association," *The Harbinger*, 2 (1845), 32.

12. "Fourierism and the Socialists," *The Dial*, 3 (1842), 87. Cf. Emerson's *Letters*, II, 361.

13. Emerson's *Journals*, VII, 407-408.

14. Emerson's *Letters*, II, 368-71.

15. Ibid., II, 371.

16. Ibid., II, 372.

17. Ibid., II, 394.

18. Ibid., II, 389.

19. Emerson's *Journals*, VII, 387.

20. *The Journal of Henry D. Thoreau*, ed. Bradford Torrey and Francis H. Allen, 14 vols. (Boston, 1906), I, 220.

21. Emerson's *Journals*, VIII, 173.

22. Ibid., VIII, 440.

23. Nathaniel Hawthorne, *The American Notebooks*, ed. Claude M. Simpson (Columbus, Ohio, 1972), p. 371.

24. Emerson's *Letters*, III, 162.

25. Emerson's *Journals*, VIII, 310.

26. According to one account — by the lady herself — Wright tried to withdraw his funds from the Fruitlands project, but Lane would not give them up to a "fallen" comrade. See Mary S. Gove Nichols's fictionalized autobiography, *Mary Lyndon* (New York, 1855), p. 218, where Lynde is Wright, Lang is Lane, and Mooney is Alcott.

27. Letter from Charles Lane to his friend in England, William Oldham, 16 June 1843. This and other letters from Lane are quoted from a typescript, "Bronson Alcott's English Friends," by William Harry Harland, in the Fruitlands Museums at Harvard, Massachusetts. I am grateful to the director of the museums, Mr. William Henry Harrison, and to Mr. Gerald Savory, great-grandson of Charles Lane, for permission to quote from them here. Some of these letters were published at the time in the *New Age* and reprinted in Clara Endicott Sears's *Bronson Alcott's Fruitlands* (Boston, 1915).

28. Lane to Oldham, 29 September 1843.

29. *The Letters of A. Bronson Alcott*, ed. Richard L. Herrnstadt (Ames, Iowa, 1969), p. 107.

30. An unpublished passage from Alcott's "Diary" for January 1847. Quoted by permission of Mrs. F. W. Pratt, and of the Houghton Library at Harvard, where the manuscript is part of the Alcott Collections.

31. Lane to Oldham, 28 June 1843.

32. Lane to Oldham, 30 July 1843.

33. Mrs. Alcott's diary for the Fruitlands period is printed in Alcott's *Journals*, p. 153.

34. Sears, p. 78.

35. *Louisa May Alcott: Her Life, Letters, and Journals*, ed. Ednah D. Cheney (Boston, 1889), p. 37.

36. Lane to Oldham, 29 September 1843.

37. Emerson's *Journals*, VIII, 433.

38. Emerson's *Letters*, III, 196.

39. Emerson's *Journals*, IX, 11.

40. Ibid., VIII, 38.

41. Margaret Fuller to Richard Fuller, 25 May 1841, quoted in *Margaret Fuller: American Romantic*, ed. Perry Miller (Garden City, N. Y., 1963), p. 75.

42. Emerson's *Journals*, VII, 420.

43. *The Correspondence of Henry David Thoreau*, ed. Walter Harding and Carl Bode (New York, 1958), p. 115.

44. *The Journals of Bronson Alcott*, ed. Odell Shepard (Boston, 1938), p. 238.

45. "Historic Notes of Life and Letters in New England," *The Complete Works of Ralph Waldo Emerson*, ed. Edward Waldo Emerson, 12 vols. (Boston and New York, 1903-1904), X, 356.

46. Thoreau's *Journal*, I, 311.

47. Emerson's *Journals*, VII, 525.

48. Alcott's *Journals*, p. 181.

49. Emerson's *Letters*, III, 230..

50. Alcott's *Letters*, pp. 107-108.

51. Lane to Oldham, 29 September 1843.

52. Lane to Oldham, 30 October 1843.

53. Emerson's *Letters*, III, 214.

54. *Louisa May Alcott*, p. 38.

55. Lane to Oldham, 16 June 1843.
56. Lane to Oldham, 30 October 1843.
57. Alcott's *Journals*, p. 155.
58. Lane to Oldham, 30 August 1843.
59. Lane to Oldham, 26 and 29 November 1843.
60. Emerson's *Journals*, IX, 50.
61. Emerson's *Letters*, III, 230.
62. Lane to Oldham, 26 and 29 November 1843.
63. Ibid.
64. Alcott's *Letters*, p. 109.
65. Alcott's *Journals*, p. 156.
66. Emerson's *Letters*, III, 262.
67. Ibid., III, 263n.
68. Alcott's *Letters*, p. 117; Emerson's *Letters*, IV, 234.
69. Alcott's *Journals*, p. 206.
70. F. B. Sanborn and William T. Harris, *A. Bronson Alcott: His Life and Philosophy*, 2 vols. (Boston, 1893), II, 430.
71. *The Correspondence of Emerson and Carlyle*, ed. Joseph Slater (New York, 1964), p. 399.
72. Ibid., p. 369.
73. Alcott's *Journals*, p. 179.
74. Ibid., p. 197.
75. Emerson's *Letters*, III, 411.
76. Edward Waldo Emerson, *Emerson in Concord* (Boston, 1889), pp. 127-28.
77. Alcott's *Journals*, p. 178.
78. Ibid., p. 184.
79. Ibid., p. 204.
80. *Walden*, ed. J. Lyndon Shanley (Princeton, N.J., 1971), p. 137.
81. Emerson's *Journals*, VII, 463.
82. *Walden*, p. 135.
83. Emerson's *Journals*, IX, 236.
84. *Walden*, pp. 134-35.
85. Thoreau's *Journal*, II, 43.
86. Emerson's *Journals*, VIII, 10-11.
87. Ibid., V, 34.
88. Quoted in James Elliot Cabot, *A Memoir of Ralph Waldo Emerson*, 2 vols. (Boston, 1887), II, 436-38.
89. *Walden*, p. 58.
90. Ibid., p. 98
91. Emerson's *Journals*, VII, 526.
92. Thoreau's *Journal*, I, 241-42.
93. *Walden*, p. 5.
94. Thoreau's *Journal*, I, 244.
95. Ibid., I, 299.
96. *Walden*, p. 46.
97. "Man the Reformer," p. 148.

98. Ibid., p. 149.

99. Lane to Oldham, 28 June 1843.

100. Emerson's *Journals*, IX, 99.

101. "Man the Reformer," p. 152.

102. *Passages from the American Note-Books*, Vol. IX in *The Complete Works of Nathaniel Hawthorne*, ed. George P. Lathrop, 12 vols. (Boston, 1882-83), IX, 229.

103. Emerson's *Journals*, IX, 10.

104. *A Lecture on Association, in Its Connection with Religion* (Boston, 1844), p. 26.

105. Emerson's *Journals*, IX, 100.

106. *Walden*, p. 33.

107. Emerson's *Journals*, IX, 54-55.

108. Quoted in Frothingham, *George Ripley*, from Ripley's invitation to Emerson.

109. Emerson's *Journals*, IX, 226.

110. "Man the Reformer," p. 148.

111. Albert Brisbane, *Social Destiny of Man* (Philadelphia, 1840), p. 29.

112. Letter from Lane to Mrs. Alcott, 22 February 1845; manuscript in the Fruitlands Museums.

113. "Social Tendencies," *The Dial*, 4 (1843), 72.

114. "Brook Farm." *The Dial*, 4 (1844), 352, 354.

115. "Millenial Church," *The Dial*, 4 (1844), 537.

116. Letter from Lane to Mrs. Alcott, 22 February 1845, quoted above.

117. Emerson's *Journals*, IX, 63.

118. Letter from Lane to Junius Alcott, 7 March 1843; manuscript in the Fruitlands Museums.

119. Emerson's *Letters*, III, 41.

120. Emerson's *Journals*, IX, 61.

121. See *The Present*, 1 (1844), 288.

122. Lane to Junius Alcott, 7 March 1843, quoted above.

123. "Social Tendencies," p. 200.

124. "Brook Farm," p. 355.

125. "The True LIfe," *The Present,* 1 (1844), 315-16.

126. Ibid., p. 315.

127. Alcott's *Journals*, p. 158.

128. Ibid., pp. 154, 156.

129. Alcott's *Letters*, p. 119.

130. The "childhood family" would have been symbolic only, of course; Bronson and Junius were too far apart in age to have been children together. No doubt their mother, who lived with Junius, figured significantly in Alcott's new vision of a "Holy Family."

131. Alcott's *Letters*, pp. 125-26.

132. Ibid., p. 656.

133. Cabot, II, 437, 438.

134. Emerson's *Journals*, IX, 63.

135. Ibid., IX, 62.
136. Ibid., IX, 114.
137. Ibid., IX, 163.
138. "Man the Reformer," p. 153.
139. Emerson's *Journals*, VII, 420.
140. Ibid., VIII, 267; *Walden*, p. 98.
141. Emerson's *Journals*, VII, 526.
142. Ibid., IX, 226.
143. "Man the Reformer," p. 153.
144. "Life in the Woods," *The Dial*, 4 (1844), 422.
145. Ibid., pp. 423-24.
146. Ibid., p. 422.
147. *Walden*, p. 82.
148. Emerson's *Journals*, VII, 144.
149. Ibid.
150. Thoreau's *Journal*, II, 406.
151. Thoreau's *Correspondence*, p. 265.
152. "Life in the Woods," p. 423.
153. *The Harbinger*, 2 (1846), 265.
154. Ibid.
155. Alcott's *Journals*, p. 185.
156. An unpublished passage in Alcott's "Diary" for 29 November 1849, quoted by permission of Mrs. F. W. Pratt, and of the Houghton Library at Harvard, where the manuscript is part of the Alcott Collections.
157. *Correspondence of Emerson and Carlyle*, p. 326.
158. *The Maine Woods*, ed. Joseph J. Moldenhauer (Princeton, N.J., 1972), p. 65.
159. Ibid., p. 68.
160. Thoreau's *Journal*, II, 328-29.
161. Ibid.

Notes to Food for Thought

1. "Social Tendencies," *The Dial*, 4 (1843), 197.
2. "Introductory Lecture," *Nature, Addresses, and Lectures*, vol. 1 of *The Collected Works of Ralph Waldo Emerson*, ed. Robert E. Spiller and Alfred R. Ferguson (Cambridge, Mass., 1971-), pp. 179-80.
3. *The Journals and Miscellaneous Notebooks of Ralph Waldo Emerson*, ed. William H. Gilman, Alfred R. Ferguson, et al. (Cambridge, Mass., 1960-), VIII, 126.
4. "Historic Notes of Life and Letters in New England," *The Complete Works of Ralph Waldo Emerson*, ed. Edward Waldo Emerson, 12 vols. (Boston and New York, 1903-1904), X, 326.

5. Ibid., p. 329.

6. Ibid., p. 356.

7. Letter from Charles Lane to William Oldham, 30 July 1843, quoted from "Bronson Alcott's English Friends," by William Harry Harland, typescript in the Fruitlands Museums.

8. Letter from Marianne Dwight to Anna Parsons, 14 December 1844, in *Letters from Brook Farm 1844-1847 by Marianne Dwight*, ed. Amy L. Reed (Poughkeepsie, N. Y., 1928), p. 51.

9. Emerson's *Journals*, VII, 351.

10. Ibid., VIII, 406.

11. Ibid., IV, 5, 266. On this early repugnance see Evelyn Barish (Greenberger), "The Phoenix on the Wall: Consciousness in Emerson's Early and Late Journals," *American Transcendental Quarterly*, No. 21 (Winter 1974), 45-56.

12. Emerson's *Journals*, IX, 277.

13. Ibid., VII, 492.

14. Ibid., IX, 383; VII, 497.

15. *Walden*, ed. J. Lyndon Shanley (Princeton, N.J., 1971), p. 61.

16. *The Journal of Henry D. Thoreau*, ed. Bradford Torrey and Francis H. Allen, 14 vols. (Boston, 1906), VI, 20.

17. *The Correspondence of Henry David Thoreau*, ed. Walter Harding and Carl Bode (New York, 1958), pp. 508 and 623. Thoreau told Emerson that "12 lbs. of Indian meal, which one can easily carry on his back will be food for a fortnight" (Emerson's *Journals*, X, 151).

18. *Walden*, p. 61.

19. Ibid., p. 214.

20. Ibid., p. 218.

21. Sandford Salyer, *Marmee, the Mother of Little Women* (Norman, Okla., 1949), p. 73.

22. "The Consociate Family Life" was published in many newspapers and journals, including *The Herald of Freedom, The Liberator, The New Age, The New York Weekly Tribune*, and *The Dial*. It is conveniently reprinted in Clara Endicott Sears, *Bronson Alcott's Fruitlands* (Boston, 1915), pp. 41-52.

23. *The Journals of Bronson Alcott*, ed. Odell Shepard (Boston, 1938), p. 146.

24. *The Correspondence of Emerson and Carlyle*, ed. Joseph Slater (New York, 1964), pp. 330-31.

25. Quoted in Odell Shepard, *Pedlar's Progress: The Life of Bronson Alcott* (Boston, 1937), p. 397.

26. Bronson Alcott, *Tablets* (Boston, 1868), p. 36; Alcott's *Journals*, p. 488.

27. Alcott's *Journals*, p. 115.

28. Lane to Oldham, 16 June and 30 July 1843.

29. Sears, p. 91.

30. *The Letters of A. Bronson Alcott*, ed. Richard L. Herrnstadt (Ames, Iowa, 1969), p. 97.

31. Lane to Oldham, 2 February and 1 March 1843.

32. *Tablets*, p. 36.

33. *The Early Lectures of Ralph Waldo Emerson*, ed. Stephen Whicher, Robert Spiller, Wallace Williams, 3 vols. (Cambridge, Mass., 1959-72), III, 262.

34. Alcott's *Journals*, p. 131.

35. Ibid., p. 132.

36. Ibid., p. 63.

37. Ibid., p. 236.

38. Thoreau's *Journal*, I, 226.

39. Emerson's *Journals*, IX, 433.

40. April 1847. This passage is not included in the published journals. It is quoted with the kind permission of Mrs. F. W. Pratt, and of the Houghton Library at Harvard, where the manuscript resides.

41. Emerson's *Journals*, X, 113.

42. Thoreau's *Journal*, I, 79.

43. Thoreau's *Correspondence*, p. 161.

44. *Parables and Paradoxes*, ed. Nahum N. Glatzer (New York, 1961), p. 187.

45. Thoreau's *Journal*, I, 149.

46. *Walden*, p. 210.

47. Thoreau's *Journal*, I, 227.

48. Emerson's *Journals*, IX, 334.

49. *Walden*, pp. 214-15.

50. Thoreau's *Journal*, I, 372.

51. Perry Miller, *Consciousness in Concord* (Boston, 1958), pp. 124-25.

52. Thoreau's *Journal*, III, 5.

53. Ibid., II, 391.

54. Ibid., I, 316.

55. Emerson's *Journals*, VIII, 282.

56. "Reminiscences of Brook Farm," *Old and New Boston*, 3 (1871), 437.

57. *Pedlar's Progress*, p. 441.

58. *The Basic Writings of Sigmund Freud*, ed. and trans. A. A. Brill (New York, 1938), p. 860.

59. Emerson's *Journals*, VII, 318; *Early Lectures*, III, 260-61.

60. Ibid., VII, 500.

61. Ibid., VIII, 155.

62. *The Conduct of Life*, Emerson's *Works* 1903 edn., VI, 154.

63. Alcott's *Journals*, p. 60.

64. Thoreau's *Journal*, I, 34-35.

65. Emerson's *Journals*, VIII, 126.

66. Note in Emerson's *Works* 1903 edn., VI, 376.

67. Emerson's *Journals*, VII, 458.

68. Ibid., VII, 131.

69. Ibid., VIII, 199.

70. Ibid., IX, 394.

71. *Walden*, p. 210.

72. Ibid., pp. 217-18.
73. Ibid., p. 216.
74. Thoreau's *Journal*, II, 143.
75. Emerson's *Journals*, IX, 101-102.

Notes to "New Modes of Thinking"

1. *The Journals and Miscellaneous Notebooks of Ralph Waldo Emerson*, ed. William H. Gilman, Alfred R. Ferguson, et al. (Cambridge, Mass., 1960-), V, 237.
2. Ibid., XIII, 141; *Walden*, ed. J. Lyndon Shanley (Princeton, N.J. 1971), p. 3.
3. *The Correspondence of Henry David Thoreau*, ed. Walter Harding and Carl Bode (New York, 1958), p. 265.
4. Emerson's *Journals*, X, 154.
5. Ibid., X, 326.
6. Quoted in *Autobiography of Brook Farm*, ed. Henry W. Sams (Englewood Cliffs, N. J., 1958), p. 35.
7. Emerson's *Journals*, X, 110.
8. "Man the Reformer," *Nature, Addresses, and Lectures*, vol. 1 of *The Collected Works of Ralph Waldo Emerson*, ed. Robert E. Spiller and Alfred R. Ferguson (Cambridge, Mass., 1971-), p. 153.
9. *The Journal of Henry D. Thoreau*, ed. Bradford Torrey and Francis H. Allen, 14 vols. (Boston, 1906), I, 312.
10. Emerson's *Journals*, XIII, 66.

Index

Index

175

Times," 17-18, 118; "Man the Reformer," 13, 19, 69, 73, 93-94; *Memoirs of Margaret Fuller Ossoli*, 25-26; *Nature*, 13, 18-19, 32; "New England Reformers," 69; "Politics," 19, 56, 157; "The Transcendentalist," 17-18; "War," 57-59
Emerson, Waldo, 77-78, 86, 139
Emerson, William, 76
Everett, Abram, 94

family, 39, 49, 84-85, 93-94, 101-10, 149-50, 152-53
Farley, Frank, 96
Finney, Charles G., 27
Foster, Stephen, 28
Fourierism,72, 74-75, 96-101, 111, 121
Freud, Sigmund, 136
Fruitlands, 14, 21, 40, 43, 45, 48-49, 52, 78-87, 94, 99-104, 113, 119-21, 124-25, 129-30, 132, 156, 165-66
Fugitive Slave Act, 29-30, 40, 43-44
Fuller, Margaret, *see* Ossoli, Margaret Fuller

Gandhi, Mohandas K., 147, 156
Garrison, William Lloyd, 27, 29-31, 33, 36, 40-42, 48, 52, 57, 63, 147, 164
Goodman, Paul, 146-47
Gove, Mary S., *see* Nichols, Mary S. Gove
Greeley, Horace, 27, 29
Growing Up Absurd (Goodman), 146

Hawthorne, Nathaniel, 13-15, 20, 41, 77, 96, 109, 119, 153; *The Blithedale Romance*, 15, 96; "The Gray Champion," 41; *The Scarlet Letter*, 13
Hecker, Isaac, 80, 82, 105
Helps, Arthur, 55
Higginson, Thomas Wentworth, 40-42, 122
"Hillside, The," 14, 86-87, 99, 109
Hoar, Edward, 45

Hoar, Elizabeth, 45
Hoar, Rockwood, 47
Hoar, "Squire" Samuel, 45, 47, 50, 51
Holmes, Oliver Wendell, 27
homesteading, *see* agrarianism
Hopedale Community, 40, 102
huts, 86-94, 108, 156

imagination, *see* consciousness
individualism, 150-51

Jefferson, Thomas, 157
journal-keeping, 37, 110, 119-20, 123, 128-29, 137-42, 149, 154

Kafka, Franz, 131
Kelly, Abby, 28
King, Martin Luther, 146, 156
Kirby, Georgiana Bruce, 135

Ladd, William, 48
Lane, Charles, 39-40, 43, 45-48, 52, 76, 78-80, 82-86, 94, 99-104, 107-12, 117, 121-22, 125-27, 135, 152-53, 156, 165; "Life in the Woods," 108; "Social Tendencies," 99, 102, 117
Lane, William, 78
Larned, Samuel, 80, 94
lecturing, 28-29
Liberation, 148
Liberator, The, 48, 52

manual labor, 70-73, 76, 81-82, 91-93, 96-99, 106-07, 150, 153
May, Samuel J., 43, 50
media, 146, 149, 156-57
Melville, Herman, 13-15, 20-21, 111-13; "Bartleby," 21, 131; *Billy Budd, 21; Moby-Dick*, 13, 21; *Typee*, 15, 111-13
Mexican War, 45, 49-51, 53-54
Miller, Perry, 64, 133
Millerites, 27
Modern Times, N. Y., 120
Mormonism, 28
"movement" politics, 146, 151